Becker Professional Education, a global leader in professional education, has been developing study materials for ACCA for more than 20 years, and thousands of candidates studying for the ACCA Qualification have succeeded in their professional examinations through its Platinum and Gold ALP training centers in Central and Eastern Europe and Central Asia.*

Becker Professional Education has also been awarded ACCA Approved Content Provider Status for materials for the Diploma in International Financial Reporting (DipIFR).

Nearly half a million professionals have advanced their careers through Becker Professional Education's courses. Throughout its more than 50-year history, Becker has earned a strong track record of student success through world-class teaching, curriculum and learning tools.

We provide a single destination for individuals and companies in need of global accounting certifications and continuing professional education.

Platinum – Moscow, Russia and Kiev, Ukraine. Gold – Almaty, Kazakhstan

Becker Professional Education's ACCA Study Materials

All of Becker's materials are authored by experienced ACCA lecturers and are used in the delivery of classroom courses.

Study System: Gives complete coverage of the syllabus with a focus on learning outcomes. It is designed to be used both as a reference text and as part of integrated study. It also includes the ACCA Syllabus and Study Guide, exam advice and commentaries and a Study Question Bank containing practice questions relating to each topic covered.

Revision Question Bank: Exam style and standard questions together with comprehensive answers to support and prepare students for their exams. The Revision Question Bank also includes past examination questions (updated where relevant), model answers and alternative solutions and tutorial notes.

Revision Essentials*: A condensed, easy-to-use aid to revision containing essential technical content and exam guidanc€

Revision Essentials are substantially derived from content reviewed by ACCA's examining team.

Substantially derived from content
reviewed by ACCA's examining team

BE

PROFESSI

ACCA

PAPER F7

FINANCIAL REPORTING
(INTERNATIONAL)

REVISION ESSENTIALS

For Examinations to June 2016

This training material has been published and prepared by Becker Professional Development International Limited

16 Elmtree Road
Teddington
TW11 8ST
United Kingdom.

ISBN: 978-1-78566-112-9

For more information about any of Becker's materials, please visit our website at www.becker-atc.com or email acca@becker.com.

CONTENTS

CAUTION: These notes offer guidance on key issues.
Reliance on these alone is insufficient to pass the examination

Aim

To develop knowledge and skills in understanding and applying accounting standards and the theoretical framework in the preparation of financial statements of entities, including groups and how to analyse and interpret those financial statements.

Main capabilities

On successful completion of this paper, candidates should be able to:

A   Discuss and apply a conceptual and regulatory frameworks for financial reporting

B   Account for transactions in accordance with International accounting standards

C   Analyse and interpret financial statements.

D   Prepare and present financial statements for single entities and business combinations in accordance with International accounting standards.

Syllabus structure

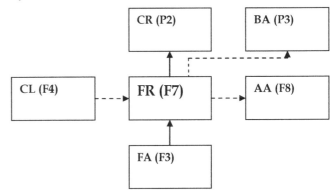

Exam format

- ✓ 3 hour paper-based examination.

- ✓ Additional 15 minutes reading and planning time.

- ✓ All questions are compulsory.

- ✓ Both computational and discursive elements. Some questions will adopt a scenario/case study approach.

  - ➢ Section A: 20 MCQs of 2 marks each.

  - ➢ Section B: two 15-mark and one 30-mark question.

- ✓ The 30 mark question will examine the preparation of financial statements for either a single entity or a group.

- ✓ Section A and the other two questions in section B can cover *any* area of the syllabus.

- ✓ A question may relate to more than one syllabus area.

- ✓ An understanding of accounting principles and concepts and how these are applied to practical examples will be tested.

- ✓ Questions on topic areas that are also included in Paper F3 will be examined at an appropriately greater depth in F7.

- ✓ Candidates will be expected to appreciate:

  - ➢ the need for specified standards and why they have been issued; and

  - ➢ the principles and key elements of complex standards.

Examinable documents

The documents listed as examinable can be found at http://www.accaglobal.com/gb/en/student/exam-support-resources/fundamentals-exams-study-resources/f7/examinable-documents.html.

These are the latest that were issued prior to 1st September 2014 and will be examinable in the September 2015 to June 2016 examination sessions.

CORE TOPICS

Tick when completed

Conceptual and regulatory framework

- ✓ Qualitative characteristics ☐
- ✓ Recognition and measurement ☐
- ✓ Fair value ☐

Accounting for transactions in financial statements

- ✓ Tangible non-current assets ☐
- ✓ Intangible non-current assets ☐
- ✓ Impairment of assets ☐
- ✓ Inventory and biological assets ☐
- ✓ Financial instruments ☐
- ✓ Leasing ☐
- ✓ Provisions ☐
- ✓ Events after the reporting period ☐
- ✓ Taxation ☐
- ✓ Reporting financial performance ☐
- ✓ Revenue ☐
- ✓ Government grants ☐

CORE TOPICS

Tick when completed

Analysis and interpreting financial statements

- ✓ Calculation and interpretation of ratios ☐

Preparation of financial statements

- ✓ Single entity ☐
- ✓ Statement of cash flows ☐
- ✓ Consolidated, including an associate ☐

(v)

1 ACCOUNTING PRINCIPLES

1.1 What is GAAP?

✓ GAAP = Generally Accepted Accounting Principles.

✓ A set of financial accounting standards and reporting guidelines used to prepare accounts.

✓ May or may not have legal authority.

✓ A dynamic concept.

1.2 Sources of GAAP

✓ Regulatory framework

  ➢ Statute (e.g. Companies Acts)
  ➢ Accounting standards

    – IFRSs
    – UK FRSs
    – USA FASs

✓ Other sources

  ➢ Best practice
  ➢ Industry groups.

2 IASB

2.1 Objective

✓ To develop, in the public interest, a <u>single set</u> of <u>high quality</u>, global accounting standards.

✓ To promote their use and rigorous application.

✓ To promote adoption of IFRSs.

2.2 Standard setting

Due process (mandatory steps)

Consult advisory council to add topic to agenda

↓

Publish an ED for comment

↓

Consider comments received in comment period

↓

Approval of standard

3   IFRS

3.1   GAAP hierarchy

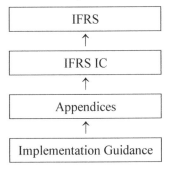

3.2   General purpose financial statements

- ✓ Published financial statements of all profit-oriented entities.
- ✓ Aimed at common information needs of many users.
- ✓ Individual entity and consolidated financial statements.

4   NOT-FOR-PROFIT ORGANISATIONS

4.1   Primary objectives

- ✓ Is not profitability!
- ✓ Is usually not financial.
- ✓ Usually to meet needs of members of society (e.g. in health and education).

1 PURPOSE AND SCOPE

1.1 Purpose

- ✓ To help users/auditors/preparers of FS understand the basis of preparation.

- ✓ To help countries develop their own national standards.

- ✓ To assist the IASB in developing consistent standards.

1.2 Scope

- ✓ Objectives of FS
- ✓ Underlying assumption
- ✓ Qualitative characteristics
- ✓ Definitions, recognition and measurement of elements
- ✓ Concepts of capital and capital maintenance

2 GENERAL PURPOSE FINANCIAL REPORTING

2.1 Objective

- ✓ To provide *information* about:

  - ➢ Financial position (e.g. solvency) $\Rightarrow SoFP$
  - ➢ Financial performance (e.g. profitability) $\Rightarrow SoCI$
  - ➢ Cash flows $\Rightarrow CFS$

- ✓ To show results of management's stewardship ("accountability").

2.2 Financial Position, Performance and Changes in Financial Position

Financial position

- ✓ Affected by:

  - ➢ economic resources controlled;
  - ➢ financial structure;
  - ➢ liquidity and solvency;
  - ➢ capacity to adapt to changes.

Financial performance

- ✓ In particular profitability.

- ✓ To predict capacity to generate cash flows from existing resource base.

- ✓ To form judgements about effectiveness with which additional resources might be employed.

Changes in financial position

- ✓ To evaluate investing, financing and operating activities.

- ✓ To assess ability to generate cash flows.

- ✓ To indicate how cash is obtained and spent.

2.3 Underlying assumption

Going concern

✓ The entity will continue in operation for the foreseeable future.

✓ No intention or need to liquidate or significantly curtail the scale of operations.

3 QUALITATIVE CHARACTERISTICS

Attributes that make information useful to users.

3.1 "Economic phenomena"

✓ **Transactions**, **conditions** and other **events** that affect economic resources and claims against the entity.

3.2 Fundamental qualitative characteristics

Relevance

✓ Helps users:
  ➢ evaluate past, present or future events; and
  ➢ confirm or correct past evaluations.

✓ Is affected by:
  ➢ nature (alone may be insufficient to be relevant);
  ➢ materiality.

"Information is <u>material</u> if its omission or misstatement could influence the economic decisions of users taken on the basis of the financial statements."

✓ Depends on size ... omission or misstatement.

✓ A "threshold" or "cut-off point" (not a primary qualitative characteristic).

Faithful representation

✓ Financial statements represent economic phenomena in words and numbers. Encompasses:
  ➢ Neutrality (free from *material* bias).
  ➢ Completeness (within materiality/cost constraints).
  ➢ Accuracy (free from *material* error).

3.3 Enhancing qualitative characteristics

✓ Comparability – Accounting bases, etc (over time and between companies).

✓ Verifiability – different parties could reach same consensus through direct or indirect means.

✓ Timeliness – available in time for users to make decisions.

✓ Understandability – presenting information clearly and concisely. Difficulty is not grounds for exclusion.

4 ELEMENTS OF FINANCIAL STATEMENTS

4.1 Terminology

✓ Asset

- ➢ Control
- ➢ Past event
- ➢ Inflow of future economic benefits

✓ Liability

- ➢ Present obligation
- ➢ Past event
- ➢ Outflow of future economic benefits

✓ Equity

- ➢ Assets less liabilities

✓ Income

- ➢ Increases in economic benefits
- ➢ Due to increase in assets/decrease in liabilities
- ➢ Resulting in increase in equity
- ➢ Other than contribution by equity shareholders

✓ Expense

- ➢ Decreases in economic benefits
- ➢ Due to decrease in assets/increase in liabilities
- ➢ Resulting in decrease in equity
- ➢ Other than distribution to equity shareholders

4.2 Recognition

✓ Meaning – incorporating in FS an item which meets the definition and the criteria.

✓ Criteria

- ➢ **Probable** future economic benefits; **and**
- ➢ **Reliable measurement** of cost/value.

4.3 Measurement

Bases

✓ Historical cost – at acquisition
✓ Current cost – current amount
✓ Realisable value – on sale or settlement
✓ Present value – discounted

5 CAPITAL AND MAINTENANCE

5.1 Historical cost accounting

Advantages		*Disadvantages*	
✓	Easy to understand	✗	Matched with current revenues
✓	Objective evidence	✗	Asset values ≠ economic benefits
✓	Widely used	✗	Holding/operating gains not separated.

5.2 Concepts of capital

✓ Capital = equity

✓ Two concepts

➢ Financial capital maintenance ⇒ Profit if closing net assets ≥ opening net assets

➢ Physical capital maintenance ⇒ Profit if physical productive capacity increases over the period

6 FAIR VALUE

The price that would be received ... or paid ... in an orderly transaction between market participants at measurement date.

6.1 Non-financial assets

✓ Fair value reflects its "highest and best" use:

➢ use which is physically possible;

➢ what is legally allowed; and

➢ the financial feasibility of using the asset.

6.2 Valuation techniques

✓ **Market** approach – uses prices, etc, generated in a market of identical or comparable assets or liabilities.

✓ **Cost** approach – to replace the service capacity of the asset (current replacement cost).

✓ **Income** approach – discounts future cash flows to a current value (e.g. present value).

6.3 Hierarchy of inputs

✓ Level 1 input – quoted (unadjusted) prices in active market for identical item that entity can access at measurement date.

✓ Level 2 input – inputs other that quoted prices within Level 1 that are observable for the item, either directly or indirectly.

✓ Level 3 input – unobservable inputs for the item.

6.4 Disclosure

✓ Quantitative and qualitative.
✓ Recurring and non-recurring
✓ Reason for using fair value.
✓ Level of hierarchy used.

1 FINANCIAL STATEMENTS

✓ Objectives – as per the *Conceptual Framework.*

2 OVERALL CONSIDERATIONS

Assumed knowledge from F3/FFA *Financial Accounting:*

✓ Faithful representation

✓ Compliance with IFRSs – must be **disclosed**

✓ Departure from IFRS – is **extremely rare**

✓ Going concern – minimum 12 months foreseeable future

✓ Accrual basis – is not the same as "matching" concept

✓ Consist presentation – changes must be **disclosed**

✓ Materiality (disclose separately) and aggregation (immaterial amounts)

✓ Off-setting –prohibited unless required/allowed

✓ Comparative information – one year minimum.

3 STRUCTURE AND CONTENT

3.1 "Disclosure"

✓ Encompassing items presented in each financial statement as well as notes.

3.2 Identification of financial statements

Must be clearly identified and distinguished from other information (e.g. in annual report)

3.3 Reporting date and period

✓ At least annually.

4 STATEMENT OF FINANCIAL POSITION

4.1 Current/non-current distinction

✓ Distinction must generally be made.
✓ *Unless* liquidity basis is reliable and more relevant.

4.2 "Current"

Asset	Liability
✓ In the normal course of the operating cycle	✓ In the normal course of the operating cycle
✓ Primarily for trading purposes	✓ Primarily for trading purposes
✓ Realisation expected within 12 months	✓ Settlement expected within 12 months
✓ Cash/cash equivalents	✓ No unconditional right to defer

5 STATEMENT OF COMPREHENSIVE INCOME

5.1 Presentation

✓ In a *single* statement of comprehensive income; or

✓ In *two* statements:

  ➢ Profit or loss for period; and
  ➢ Other comprehensive income.

✓ Profit or loss and total comprehensive income attributed to:

  ➢ non-controlling interest; and
  ➢ owners of the parent.

5.2 Profit or loss

✓ Total income less expenses excluding items of other comprehensive income.

5.3 Other comprehensive income

✓ Revaluation surplus for period.

✓ Gains from financial assets at fair value through other comprehensive income.

✓ Certain exchange differences.

✓ Deferred tax relating to above.

5.4 Material items

✓ Disclose separately.

5.5 Analysis of expenses

✓ Classification by nature or by function.

6 STATEMENT OF CHANGES IN EQUITY

6.1 Separate statement

✓ Must show:

  ➢ Total comprehensive income for the period (attributable to parent and non-controlling interest);

  ➢ Effects of changes in accounting policy and corrections of errors (IAS 8);

  ➢ Dividends and other transaction with owners (e.g. share issues);

  ➢ Reconciliation of carrying amounts (i.e. b/f $\pm$ movements = c/f).

6.2 Reclassification to profit or loss

✓ May be prohibited (e.g. revaluation surplus on property).

✓ May be required (e.g. on derecognition of financial assets measured at fair value through other comprehensive income).

7 NOTES

7.1 Structure

✓ Basis of preparation and accounting policies

✓ Information required by IFRS not on face of FS

✓ Additional information relevant to understanding

7.2 Disclosure of significant accounting policies

✓ Measurement bases used.

✓ Other relevant policies.

✓ Judgements made in applying policies.

7.3 Key sources of estimation uncertainty

✓ Include key assumptions about the future.

✓ Disclose if significant risk of carrying amounts being affected in next year.

7.4 Other disclosure standards

✓ IAS 10 *Events After the Reporting Period*

✓ IFRS 5 *Non-current Assets Held for Sale and Discontinued Operations*

✓ IAS 33 *Earnings per Share*

1 IAS 8

1.1 Scope

✓ Accounting policies – *selecting*, and *changing*.
✓ *Changes* in accounting estimates
✓ *Correction* of prior period errors.

2 ACCOUNTING POLICIES

Specific principles, bases, conventions, rules and practices applied in preparing and presenting financial statements.

2.1 Selection and application

✓ Standard or Interpretation;

✓ Considering implementation guidance;

✓ Standards and interpretations dealing with similar/related issues;

✓ Framework definitions, recognition criteria and measurement concepts;

✓ Recent pronouncements of other standard-setters;

✓ Accepted industry practice (must not conflict with "The Framework")

GAAP hierarchy

2.2 Consistency

✓ Must be applied consistently to similar items unless IFRS requires or permits otherwise (e.g. categorisation of inventories).

2.3 Changes in accounting policies

✓ Only allowed if:

➢ Required by IFRS;
➢ It provides reliable and more relevant information.

✓ Initial revaluation of assets is dealt with in IAS 16 or IAS 38 *not* IAS 8.

✓ Applying changes in accounting policies:

➢ Initial application see transitional provisions (if any);

➢ Otherwise **retrospectively**.

✓ Early application is **not** a voluntary change.

Retrospective application

✓ Means as if new policy had always been applied.

➢ Restate comparatives (opening balance of each affected component of equity);

➢ From earliest practicable period.

Disclosures

- ✓ Relevant IFRS (mandatory change) and compliance with transitional provisions (if any).

- ✓ Reason for voluntary change.

- ✓ Amounts of adjustments.

- ✓ Any reason why retrospective restatement is impracticable.

3   CHANGES IN ACCOUNTING ESTIMATES

An adjustment to the carrying amount of an asset (or liability) arising from the current assessment of expected future benefits (or obligations).

- ✓ Recognise **prospectively** (include in profit or loss in period of change and/or future periods).

- ✓ Disclose nature and amount (or that future effect is impracticable) – materiality considerations apply

4   PRIOR PERIOD ERRORS

Omissions and misstatements in previous period(s) financial statements arising from failure to use/misuse information that was available or could reasonably be expected to have been obtained.

- ✓ Corrected **retrospectively** in first FS authorised for issue after discovery by restating:

  - ➢ comparatives for prior periods presented; or

  - ➢ opening balances of earliest prior period presented (if error occurred earlier).

- ✓ If impracticable to determine period-specific or cumulative effect – restate earliest period practicable (may be current period).

- ✓ Disclosure – nature of error, amount of correction, effect on EPS (if IAS 33 applies).

1 PRINCIPLES OF REVENUE RECOGNITION

1.1 IFRS 15

✓ A "five step" model.

1.2 Identify contracts with customers

Contract – an agreement that creates enforceable rights and obligations.

Customer – the party who obtain goods or services in exchange for consideration.

✓ Contract must meet five criteria:

> ➢ approved contract;
> ➢ rights and obligations identified;
> ➢ payment terms identified;
> ➢ commercial substance; and
> ➢ probable collection of consideration due.

1.3 Identify performance obligations

Performance obligation – promise to transfer distinct goods or service (or bundle) or a series of goods or services.

✓ May require unbundling of a contract (mobile phone).

1.4 Determine the transaction price

Transaction price – the amount of consideration exchanged for transfer of goods or services.

✓ Ignore sales tax (VAT).
✓ Allow for time value of money, if relevant.
✓ Include fair value of non-cash component.
✓ Deduct consideration payable to customer.

1.5 Allocate the transaction price

✓ To all separate performance obligations in proportion to stand-alone selling prices.

✓ Estimate stand-alone price if not observable.

1.6 Recognise revenue

✓ When performance obligation is satisfied by transfer to customer.

> ➢ Normally when customer gains control;
> ➢ May be over time or at a point in time.

2 PERFORMANCE OBLIGATIONS

2.1 Satisfied over time

✓ Criteria – only **ONE** to be met:

  ➢ Customer receives/consumes benefits as performed (e.g. cleaning services).

  ➢ Performance creates or enhances an asset controlled by the customer.

  ➢ Asset has **no** alternative use and right to payment for performance to date is enforceable.

✓ Progress can be measured using input or output methods.

2.2 Satisfied at a point in time

✓ If not satisfied over time.

✓ Revenue is recognised when the customer obtains control of the asset.

✓ Indicators of transfer of control:

  ➢ customer has obligation to pay for it;
  ➢ customer has legal title to it;
  ➢ physical transfer;
  ➢ transfer of significant risks/rewards of ownership;
  ➢ customer has accepted the asset.

2.3 Statement of financial position presentation

✓ **Contract liability** – an obligation to transfer goods or services for consideration received or receivable.

✓ **Contract asset** – a right to consideration for goods or services transferred.

3 MEASURING PROGRESS

3.1 Output methods

✓ Based on value to the customer of goods or services transferred to date relative to the remainder.

3.2 Input methods

✓ Based on efforts or inputs to satisfy the performance obligation relative to total expected inputs.

3.3 Cost recognition

✓ Obligations satisfied over time – expense costs as *incurred*.

4 RECOGNITION OF CONTRACT COSTS

4.1 Incremental costs of obtaining a contract

✓ Recognise as asset expected to be recovered.
✓ Otherwise expense as incurred.

4.2 Costs to fulfil a contract

✓ If not within the scope of another standard recognise as an asset if they are direct, generate/enhance resources and expected to be recoverable.

5 SPECIFIC TRANSACTIONS

5.1 Principal v agent

Principal	Controls goods or service before transfer to customer	Revenue = Gross consideration
Agent	Another party provides goods or service	Revenue = Fee or commission

Indicators of acting as agent

✓ Another party is responsible for fulfilling the contract.
✓ No inventory risk.
✓ No discretion in setting prices.
✓ Consideration is a commission.
✓ No exposure to credit risk.

5.2 Repurchase agreements

A sales contract with a promise or option to repurchase.

Forward or call option

✓ An option or *right* to repurchase an asset which the customer does not control is:

  ➢ A **lease** – if repurchase is < original selling price; or
  ➢ A **financing arrangement** – if repurchase is ≥ original selling price.

Put option

✓ An *obligation* to repurchase at the customer's request for < original selling price is:

  ➢ A **lease** – if customer has economic incentive to exercise the right; or

  ➢ A **sale with a right of return** – if no significant economic incentive.

✓ If repurchase price ≥ original selling price, account for as:

  ➢ A **financing arrangement** – if repurchase price > expected market value; or

  ➢ A **sale with a right of return** – if repurchase price ≤ expected market value (unless customer has a significant economic incentive to exercise right).

5.3 Bill-and-hold arrangements

Contract under which customer is billed for goods not yet delivered.

✓ Revenue recognised only when customer has control.

*Control criteria – **ALL** must be met*

✓ Substantive reason for the arrangement.
✓ Goods are separately identified.
✓ Goods are ready for transfer to customer.
✓ Entity cannot use or sell to another customer.

5.4 Consignments

	Dealer/distributor	*Revenue recognition*
Sale	Has control	On shipment/delivery to dealer
Consignment	Does not have control	When dealer sells to a customer or obtains control (i.e. after a specified period of time expires).

Indicators of a consignment arrangement

✓ Goods are controlled by the entity until a specified event occurs (e.g. sale to a customer or time expiry).

✓ The entity can require that goods be returned or transferred to another party;

✓ The dealer's obligation to pay for the goods is conditional on their sale (or expiry of time).

1 INVENTORY

Assumed knowledge of IAS 2 *Inventories* from F3/FFA Financial Accounting:

- ✓ Measured at lower of cost and net realisable value (NRV):

  - ➢ Cost includes purchase price + costs of conversion + other costs incurred in bringing inventories to their place and condition

  - ➢ NRV is estimated selling price less estimated costs of completion and estimated costs to sell.

- ✓ Cost formulae:

  - ➢ Specific identification (items not ordinarily interchangeable/specific projects);

  - ➢ Otherwise FIFO or weighted average.

- ✓ Recognise cost of inventories as an expense in the period they are sold.

2 BIOLOGICAL ASSETS

2.1 IAS 41 *Agriculture*

- ✓ *Biological asset* – a living animal or plant.

- ✓ *Agricultural produce* – the product harvested from a biological asset.

2.2 Recognition

- ✓ Usual asset recognition criteria.

2.3 Measurement

- ✓ At fair value less costs to sell:

  - ➢ on initial recognition; and
  - ➢ at the end of each reporting period.

- ✓ Any gain/(loss) on initial measurement is recognised in profit or loss.

- ✓ IAS 41 *presumes* that fair value can be measured reliably. Can be **rebutted only on initial** recognition if:

  - ➢ a quoted market price is not available; and
  - ➢ alternative estimates are clearly unreliable.

1 IAS 16

1.1 Definitions

✓ Assumed F3/FFA knowledge:

> ➢ Carrying amount
> ➢ Cost
> ➢ Depreciation/depreciable amount
> ➢ Useful life.

✓ Residual value – a *current* estimate of value at the end useful life.

✓ Impairment loss – excess of carrying amount over recoverable amount.

2 RECOGNITION

✓ Framework recognition criteria apply (assumed F3/FFA).

3 INITIAL MEASUREMENT

At cost.

✓ All costs of getting asset to place and condition of use.

✓ May include:

> ➢ borrowing costs (IAS 23);
> ➢ initial estimate of decommissioning (IAS 37).

Exchange of assets

✓ Fair value of asset received = fair value of asset given up (e.g. trade-in) ± any cash.

✓ Exclusions:

> ➢ transaction lacks commercial substance; or
> ➢ no reliable measurement of fair value.

4 SUBSEQUENT COSTS

4.1 Running costs

✓ Recognise day-to-day costs in profit or loss as incurred.

4.2 Part replacement

✓ Capitalise parts if criteria met (derecognise parts replaced).

✓ Similarly "major inspection"/"overhaul costs".

5 MEASUREMENT AFTER RECOGNITION

5.1 Choice of accounting policy

✓ **Cost model** – cost less accumulated depreciation and any accumulated impairment losses.

✓ **Revaluation model** – revalued amount (i.e. fair value on revaluation) less subsequent depreciation/ impairment losses.

> ➢ Must still depreciate over useful life (except land).

6 REVALUATION MODEL

6.1 Fair value

✓ Must be measurable.

✓ IFRS 13 hierarchy of inputs applies:

> ➢ Level 1 – quoted price
> ➢ Level 2 – observable price (not quoted)
> ➢ Level 3 – unobservable inputs.

6.2 Frequency

✓ Sufficient to ensure carrying amount and fair value are not *materially* different.

✓ Entire class – **but** may be performed on a rolling basis.

6.3 Accumulated depreciation

✓ Two methods:

> ➢ restate proportionately; or
> ➢ "eliminate" against gross carrying amount (and restate net).

6.4 Movement (increase/decrease)

✓ Increase ⇒ other comprehensive income (accumulated in equity as "revaluation surplus").

✓ Decrease:

> ⇒ expense in profit or loss; or
> ⇒ other comprehensive income (if previous gain).

6.5 Subsequent accounting

Transfer to retained earnings

✓ Is allowed but not required:

> ➢ Annually (depreciation difference);
> ➢ On disposal.

✗ Must **not** be "recycled" through profit or loss.

7 DEPRECIATION

✓ Assumed F3/FFA knowledge:

> ➢ systematic basis reflects consumption of benefits;
> ➢ land is not depreciable;
> ➢ many factor affect useful life;
> ➢ residual value – often immaterial;
> ➢ change in method is a change in accounting estimate;
> ➢ ceases when asset derecognised.

8 RECOVERY OF CARRYING AMOUNT

8.1 Impairment

✓ IAS 36 applies.

8.2 Compensation (e.g. insurance proceeds)

✓ Include in profit or loss when receivable.

✗ **Not** deferred income.

✗ **Cannot** reduce impairment loss or cost of new asset.

9 DERECOGNITION

Gain or loss on disposal

✓ Recognised in profit or loss (not revenue).

✓ See also:

  ➢ IAS 17 (sale and leaseback);
  ➢ IFRS 5 (non-current assets held for sale).

10 DISCLOSURES

✓ Each class

  ➢ Measurement bases
  ➢ Depreciation methods
  ➢ Useful lives or depreciation rates
  ➢ Reconciliation of carrying amounts.

✓ Other disclosures

  ➢ Restrictions on title/assets pledged as security
  ➢ Expenses on assets in the course of construction
  ➢ Contractual commitments
  ➢ Compensation from third parties.

✓ Revalued items

  ➢ Effective date of revaluation
  ➢ Whether independent valuer involved
  ➢ Capital commitments
  ➢ Revaluation surplus – movements and restrictions on distribution.

✓ Encouraged

  ➢ Carrying amount of:

    − temporarily idle assets
    − fully depreciated assets still in use
    − assets held for disposal.

  ➢ When cost model is used, the fair value of assets (if materially different).

1 BORROWING COSTS

Interest and other costs incurred in connection with the borrowing of funds.

✓ Include:

> ➢ effective interest (IFRS 9);
> ➢ finance costs in respect of finance leases (IAS 17);
>
> ➢ exchange differences on foreign currency borrowings (IAS 21);
>
> ➢ dividends on preference shares classified as debt.

2 ACCOUNTING TREATMENT

2.1 Recognition

✓ All borrowing costs that relate to a qualifying asset must be capitalised.

✓ All other borrowing costs will be expensed when incurred.

3 CAPITALISATION ISSUES

3.1 Qualifying asset

An asset that necessarily takes a substantial period of time to get ready for its intended use or sale.

✓ May include:

> ➢ Assets under construction;
> ➢ Inventories that take time to mature.

3.2 Eligible borrowing costs

✓ Capitalise to the extent they relate to qualifying assets:

> ➢ Specific borrowing – no problem;
> ➢ General borrowing – apply capitalisation rate to expenditures incurred.

✗ **Cannot** exceed amount incurred.

3.3 Commencement

✓ When borrowing costs incurred, costs incurred on asset and active development.

3.4 Suspension

✓ If no active development – unless necessary for asset to get ready for use/sale.

3.5 Cessation

✓ When asset is substantially ready for use/sale.

1 IAS 20

- ✓ Accounting for government grants.

- ✓ Disclosure of government grants and other forms of assistance.

- ✓ Does **not** deal with:

  - ✗ Income tax benefits;
  - ✗ Government ownership;
  - ✗ Agricultural grants (IAS 41 applies).

2 GOVERNMENT GRANTS

2.1 Recognition criteria

- ✓ Only when there is *reasonable assurance* that:

  - ➢ relevant conditions will be complied with; and
  - ➢ the grant will be received.

- ✓ Includes a **forgivable** loan.

2.2 IAS 20 Accounting treatment

- ✓ Systematically recognised in profit or loss on the same basis as the costs that they compensate. ("Deferred income" approach.)

- ✗ "Capital approach" is **not** allowed.

2.3 Non-monetary grants

- ✓ Account for both assets and grant at:

  - ➢ fair value; or
  - ➢ nominal cost.

2.4 Presentation

- ✓ Capital ("asset") grants – either credited against the carrying amount of the asset or as deferred income.

- ✓ Other ("income") grants – as deferred income.

2.5 Repayment

- ✓ Account for as a change in accounting estimate.

3 GOVERNMENT ASSISTANCE

Action designed to provide an economic benefit subject to certain criteria being met.

- ✓ Includes loans at below market rate of interest.

- ✓ Significant benefit should be disclosed (if financial statements would otherwise mislead users).

1   IAS 40

1.1   Definition

Property (land or buildings, or part thereof) held to earn
rentals or for capital appreciation or both.

✗   **Not** "owner-occupied" property.

2   RECOGNITION AND MEASUREMENT

✓   Measurement at recognition:

> ➢   Cost model (IAS 16) – includes transaction costs.

3   MEASUREMENT AFTER RECOGNITION:

✓   Choice between fair value and cost models.

✓   Fair value model:

> ➢   Assess fair value at the end of each reporting
> period; any gain/loss is included in profit or loss.

> ➢   Rebuttable presumption – fair value can be
> measured reliably on a continuing basis.

✓   Cost model (as IAS 16)

✓   Transfer to another classification when change in use
evidenced – may result in a change in measurement
method.

1   IAS 38

Intangible assets – identifiable non-monetary asset without physical substance.

1.1   Definition criteria

✓   Identifiability – separable or arising from a legal (e.g. contractual) right.

✓   Control – normally, but not only, enforceable in law.

✓   Future economic benefits – can be cost savings.

2   RECOGNITION AND INITIAL MEASUREMENT

2.1   Initial measurement (at cost)

✓   **Separate** acquisition – the transaction will normally verify the cost.

✓   Business **combinations** – fair value of all identifiable intangibles of subsidiary (even if not recognised by subsidiary).

✓   **Exchange** of assets – fair value or carrying amount of asset given up (if no reliable measurement of fair value).

2.2   Subsequent expenditure

✓   Will rarely meet asset recognition criteria to justify adding to cost.

3   INTERNALLY GENERATED

3.1   Goodwill

✘   **Cannot** be recognised as an asset.

3.2   Other intangibles

✓   Must capitalise (i.e. recognise as an asset) if the specific recognition criteria are *demonstrated*.

✓   Otherwise expense ("research phase" and development "phase" that does not meet asset criteria).

3.3   Specific recognition criteria

✓   Technical feasibility.
✓   Intention to use/sell.
✓   Ability to use/sell.
✓   Probable future economic benefits.
✓   Adequate resources available to complete.
✓   Reliable measurement of expenditure.

4   MEASUREMENT AFTER RECOGNITION

4.1   Cost model (usually) or revaluation model

✓   Same as property, plant and equipment but must be an **active market** if revaluation model used.

5 USEFUL LIFE

5.1 Factors

✓ Many factors determine whether useful life is:

> ➢ Finite – cannot exceed legal rights
>
> ➢ Indefinite (is *not* infinite!)
>
>> — **No** amortisation;
>> — Impairment test *at least* annually.

5.2 Finite useful lives

✓ Residual value is assumed to be **zero** unless:

> ➢ there is a commitment to purchase; or
> ➢ it can be reliably measured in an active market.

1 IFRS 5

1.1 Definitions

✓ **Component** of an entity – operations and cash flows clearly *distinguishable* from remainder of entity (operationally and for financial reporting purposes).

✓ **Discontinued operation** – a component that has been disposed of **or** is classified as held for sale **and** is:

➢ a *separate* major line of business/geographic area;
➢ part of a *single co-ordinated plan* to discontinue; or
➢ is a subsidiary acquired exclusively for resale.

✓ **Disposal group** – a group of assets (may include goodwill) to be disposed of collectively in a single transaction, and directly associated liabilities.

2 HELD FOR SALE CLASSIFICATION

2.1 Definitions

✓ A *non-current* asset (or disposal group) is classified as "held for sale" if the carrying amount will be recovered principally through a **sale** transaction rather than use.

2.2 Recognition criteria

✓ Available for *immediate* sale in *present* condition.

✓ Sale must be *highly probable*:

➢ commitment to a plan to sell;
➢ active programme to locate buyer initiated;
➢ active marketing for reasonable selling price;
➢ completed sale expected within one year;
➢ significant changes to plan are unlikely.

Non-current assets acquired exclusively for disposal

✓ Classify as held for sale on **acquisition** if:

➢ one-year criterion is met; and
➢ it is highly probable that all other criteria will be met within 3 months.

Events after the Reporting Period

✖ Classification **cannot** be used if recognition criteria are only met after period end.

✓ But ... disclose if met before financial statements are authorised for issue (i.e. non-adjusting event).

2.3 Abandoned assets

✗ **Cannot** be classified as held for sale.

✓ But ... such a disposal group is treated as a discontinued operation when it ceases to be used.

2.4 Measurement

✓ At the lower of:

> ➢ carrying amount; and
> ➢ fair value less costs to sell (discounted if expected to occur beyond one year).

✓ Measure assets and liabilities in accordance with applicable IFRSs before measuring fair value less costs to sell of the disposal group.

✓ Impairment losses (initial or subsequent) must be recognised.

✗ Do **not** depreciate/amortise.

3 PRESENTATION AND DISCLOSURE

3.1 Discontinued operations

✓ A *single amount* in profit or loss:

> ➢ post-tax profit/(loss) of discontinued operations;
> ➢ post-tax gain/(loss) recognised on:
>> − measurement to fair value less costs to sell; or
>> − disposal of the discontinued operation.

✓ *Analysed* in profit or loss (or notes):

> ➢ revenue, expenses and pre-tax profit/(loss) of discontinued operations;
> ➢ gain/(loss) recognised on:
>> − measurement to fair value less costs to sell; or
>> − disposal.

✓ Net cash flows (operating, investing and financing) must be presented.

3.2 Held for sale

✓ Separate classification (also liabilities in a disposal group).

✓ Major classes are separately disclosed.

✓ Comparative information is **not** restated.

1 IAS 36

1.1 Definitions

✓ Impairment loss – Amount by which the carrying amount exceeds recoverable amount.

✓ Recoverable amount – Higher of fair value less costs of disposal and value in use.

✓ Fair value – as per IFRS 13.

✓ Value in use – present value of estimated future cash flows associated with the asset (continuing use and disposal).

2 BASICS

2.1 All assets

✓ At end of each reporting period, assess any indication of impairment;

　➢ If any indication exists – make formal estimate of recoverable amount;

　➢ If no indications – formal estimate is *not* required, **except** for *intangible* assets:

　　– with indefinite-life; or

　　– not yet available for use.

2.2 Indications

External sources

✓ Decline in market value *significantly* more than expected.

✓ Significant adverse changes, in technological, market, economic or legal environment.

✓ Increases in market interest rates.

✓ Carrying amount of net assets exceeds entity's market capitalisation.

Internal sources

✓ Obsolescence or physical damage.

✓ Significant adverse changes in extent or manner of use.

✓ Deterioration in economic performance.

Remaining useful life, depreciation method or residual value may need to be changed even if no impairment.

3   RECOVERABLE AMOUNT

3.1   General principles

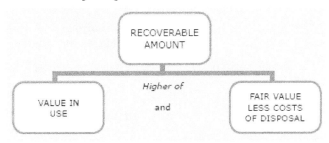

4   CGU

4.1   Basic concept

Smallest identifiable group of assets generating cash flows independently.

✓   Necessary when there is indication of impairment of an individual asset which does not generate independent cash flows.

4.2   Allocating shared assets

Goodwill acquired in a business combination

✓   Allocate to CGUs expected to benefit from synergies of business combination.

✓   Test for impairment:

➢   at least annually; or
➢   if impairment of goodwill or CGU indicated.

Corporate assets

✓   Assets other than goodwill (e.g. head office, research centre).

✓   Similarly allocate to CGUs, test for impairment and treat impairment losses as for goodwill.

5   ACCOUNTING FOR IMPAIRMENT LOSS

5.1   Basics

✓   Recoverable amount < carrying amount means that impairment has occurred:

➢   Dr Profit or loss
(or Dr Revaluation surplus in respect of the same impaired asset).
  Cr Asset
With the difference in amounts (impairment loss).

5.2 Allocation within CGU

✓ Order of allocation of impairment between assets (after accounting for any specific impairments):

- ➢ Goodwill, if any;
- ➢ Other assets on a pro-rata basis; **but**

No asset should be reduced below the **higher** of:

- − Fair value less cost of disposal;
- − Value in use;
- − Zero.

🔑 Any current assets do **not** bear any of the impairment loss as they will already be measured at a current value.

6 SUBSEQUENT REVIEW

6.1 Basics

✓ Review impaired assets each year if indications of:

- ➢ further impairment;
- ➢ impairment reversal.

6.2 Reversals of impairment losses

✓ Only reverse if original factors of impairment no longer apply.

✗ **Cannot** reverse impairment of goodwill.

✗ **Cannot** increase carrying amount to more than depreciated cost if impairment had not occurred.

1   INTRODUCTION

1.1   Definitions

✓   **Finance** lease – transfers substantially all risks and rewards incident to ownership of an asset.

✓   **Operating** lease – not a finance lease.

✓   Lease term – non-cancellable period.

✓   Fair value – exchange amount between knowledgeable and willing parties in an arm's length agreement. (≠ IFRS 13)

2   TYPE OF ARRANGEMENT

2.1   Risks and rewards of ownership

Indicators

✓   Transfer of ownership.
✓   Option to purchase.
✓   Lease term is major part of useful life.
✓   PV of minimum payment ≥ *substantially all* the fair value of the asset.

2.2   Land and buildings

✓   Account for separately (unless title to both passes at end of the lease).

3   FINANCE LEASES

3.1   Lessee accounting

✓   Capitalise asset and liability at *lower* of:

➢   PV of minimum lease payments;
➢   fair value of asset.

✓   Depreciate asset over useful life or lease term if shorter.

✓   Split repayments between capital and interest.

✓   Calculate interest using interest rate implicit in lease.

Rentals "in arrears"

✓   Every payment includes interest element.

Rentals in "advance"

✓   First payment is capital only.

3.2 Disclosures

✓ Show lease liabilities separately.

✓ Distinguish current and non-current.

✓ Minimum lease payments and their present value:

  ➤ a reconciliation; and

  ➤ analysis:

     ≤ 1 year
     1-5 years
     > 5 years

4 OPERATING LEASES

4.1 Lessee accounting

✓ Expense periodic rentals to profit or loss.

✓ Only accruals/prepayments in statement of financial position.

4.2 Disclosure

✓ Minimum lease payments under non-cancellable leases:

  ≤ 1 year
  1-5 years
  > 5 years

5 SALE AND LEASEBACK

5.1 As finance lease

✗ Do **not** derecognise asset.

✓ Restate asset to fair value.

✓ Defer any "profit" and amortise over lease term.

✓ Recognise liability, as per finance lease.

5.2 As operating lease

✓ Derecognise asset.

✓ Recognise revenue.

Profit/(loss)

✓ If selling price = fair value recognise immediately.

✓ If selling price > fair value defer and amortise over lease term.

✓ If selling price < fair value recognise immediately, unless future rentals at below market price.

1 IAS 37

1.1 Need for a standard

Uses (abuses)

- ✗ "Profit smoothing".
- ✗ "Creative accounting".
- ✗ Diverse practice ⇒ lack of comparability.
- ✗ Accounting for impairment.

1.2 Scope

- ✓ All provisions and contingencies other than the many covered by other standards.

1.3 Definitions

- ✓ **Provision** – a **liability** of uncertain timing or amount.

- ✓ **Obligating** event – creates a legal or constructive obligation (no choice but to settle).

- ✓ **Legal** obligation – contractual, statutory or other operation of law.

- ✓ **Constructive** obligation – valid expectation derives from actions:

  - ➢ Past practice;
  - ➢ Published policies or statement (of intent).

- ✓ **Contingent** liability – a past events that gives rise to:

  - ➢ a possible obligation – *existence* will be confirmed by (non-)occurrence of an uncertain future event; or

  - ➢ a present obligation which *cannot* be recognised as a liability because settlement:

    - – is not probable; or
    - – cannot be measured reliably (RARE!).

- ✓ **Contingent** asset – a possible asset arising from past events to be confirmed by an uncertain future event.

- ✓ **Onerous** contract – unavoidable costs exceed benefits.

- ✓ **Restructuring** – a planned and controlled programme to change scope or manner of business.

1.4 Provisions *v* contingent liabilities

- ✓ Distinction derived from definitions:

  - ➢ provision must be *present* obligation;
  - ➢ contingent may be present or possible.

2 RECOGNITION ISSUES

2.1 Provision

✓ **Must** be recognised when conditions are met:

➢ *present* legal or constructive obligation;
➢ as a result of *past* events;
➢ *probable* (i.e. > 50%) outflow of resources;
➢ reliable estimate.

2.2 Contingent assets and liabilities

✗ **Cannot** be recognised ...

✓ Except as required by IFRS 3.

3 MEASUREMENT

3.1 General rules

✓ **Best estimate** of amount based on.

➢ management's judgement;
➢ experience;
➢ expert (e.g. legal).

✓ Taking into account **uncertainty**:

➢ expected value (similar obligations);
➢ most likely outcome (single obligation).

✓ Other factors:

➢ time value of money (use present value);
➢ expected future events.

3.2 Specifics

✓ Recognise **reimbursement** (e.g. insurance) only when *virtually certain* (otherwise a contingent asset):

➢ expense may be presented *net*; but ...
➢ asset and liability are presented separately (i.e. *gross*).

✗ Do **not** reduce a provision by expected gains on disposal.

✓ Amount is **pre-tax**.

3.3 Changes in provision

✓ Review regular and revise up or down if estimate changes.

✓ When cash is paid out to settle the liability:

> Dr Provision (liability)
> Cr Cash (asset)

Any unused amount must be written back ("released") to profit or loss. It **cannot** be used for another purpose.

3.4 Self-insurance

✘ Setting aside a "reserve" does **not** create a provision:

➤ A transfer within equity;
➤ Actual expense in profit or loss when incurred.

4 SPECIFIC CIRCUMSTANCES

4.1 Future operating losses

✘ **Not** recognised as there is no past event.
✘ **Not** unavoidable.

4.2 Onerous contracts

The *unavoidable* costs of meeting the obligations exceed the economic benefits expected to be received from it.

✔ Present obligation relating to past event.
✔ Therefore recognise provision.

4.3 Restructurings

Examples

✔ Sale or termination of line of business
✔ Closure of business locations
✔ Relocations
✔ Changes in management structure
✔ Fundamental reorganisation

Recognition

✔ A *formal detailed plan* must identify:

➤ Business or part affected;
➤ Locations affected;
➤ Details of employees who will be compensated
➤ Expenditures to be incurred; and
➤ When it will be implemented

✔ Management must raise a *valid expectation* that restructuring will occur (e.g. by announcing it).

✘ A decision alone does **not** create a liability.

✘ There is **no** obligation to sale without a binding agreement.

✘ A provision **cannot** be made on initial acquisition of a subsidiary. (But a subsidiary can recognise before acquisition if above criteria met.)

✔ Only cost *necessarily* incurred by the restructuring that do **not** relate to ongoing activities can be included.

4.4 Decommissioning costs

✓ Recognise a provision for the present value of costs when *obligating event* occurs.

✓ Maybe on initial recognition of asset:

> Dr Non-current asset
> Cr Provision

✓ Depreciate non-current asset (including initial provision).

✓ Present value of provision increases each year:

➢ "unwinding of discount";
➢ this finance cost is charged to profit or loss.

5 REPAIRS AND MAINTENANCE

5.1 Substantial expenditure

✓ Account for in accordance with IAS 16.

✗ **No** provision – even legal requirement does **not** create liability.

6 DISCLOSURES

6.1 Each class of provision

✓ A reconciliation of carrying amounts.
✓ Brief description of obligation.
✓ An indication of uncertainties (amount or timing).
✓ Expected reimbursement (if any).

6.2 Disclosure

✓ Contingent liability – unless remote:

➢ Description of nature;
➢ If practicable:
  – Expected uncertainties;
  – Estimate of financial effect
  – Possibility of reimbursement.

✓ Similarly, contingent asset – but must be probable.

✓ Seriously prejudicial information (rare) need not be disclosed but must be explained.

1   IAS 10

Events which occur between the end of the reporting period and the date the financial statements are authorised for issue.

Two types:

- ✓ "Adjusting" – provide evidence of conditions at the end of the reporting period.

- ✓ "Non-adjusting" – indicate conditions arising after the end of the reporting period.

2   RECOGNITION AND MEASUREMENT

2.1   Adjusting events

- ✓ Financial statements are **adjusted**.

Examples

- ✓ Resolution of litigation.
- ✓ Bankruptcy of a customer.
- ✓ Discovery of fraud or error.
- ✓ Sale of inventory at less than cost.

2.2   Non-adjusting events

- ✗ **Not** adjusted.

- ✓ Disclose if "of such importance".

Examples

- ✓ Business acquisition.
- ✓ Loss through fire/flood, etc.
- ✓ Abnormal exchange rate fluctuations.
- ✓ Decline in market value of investments.

2.3   Dividends

- ✓ Proposed equity dividends (declared after the end of the reporting period) are **not** a liability at the reporting date.

2.4   Going concern

- ✓ Financial statements should **not** be prepared on a going concern basis if it is not appropriate.

3   DISCLOSURE

3.1   General

- ✓ Date financial statements were authorised for issue.
- ✓ Any power to amend after issue.

3.2   Non-adjusting events

- ✓ Nature of the event.
- ✓ Estimate of financial effect (or cannot be made).

3.3   Going concern (IAS 1)

- ✓ Financial statements are **not** prepared on this basis.
- ✓ Management's awareness of material uncertainties.

1 IAS 12

1.1 Scope

✓ Current tax
✓ Deferred tax

1.2 Definitions

✓ Accounting profit/(loss) – before deducting tax expense.

✓ Tax profit/(loss) – profit/loss on which income tax is payable/recoverable.

✓ Tax expense (income) – current plus deferred tax expense.

✓ Current tax – amount payable/recoverable for a period.

✓ Deferred tax liabilities – amounts payable in future periods in respect of *taxable temporary differences*,

✓ Deferred tax assets – amounts recoverable in future periods in respect of deductible temporary differences and unused tax losses.

✓ Tax base – the amount attributed to an asset or liability for tax purposes.

2 CURRENT TAX

2.1 Liabilities and assets

✓ Unpaid current tax is a liability.
✓ Excess of payments over amounts due is an asset.

2.2 Accounting entries

✓ Tax expense for period:

Dr	Profit or loss	$x	
	Cr Tax liability		$x

✓ When paid:

Dr	Tax liability	$x	
	Cr Cash		$x

✓ Any under/(over) provision increases/(decreases) tax expense of the following period.

3 DEFERRED TAX

3.1 Underlying problem

✓ Different tax and accounting treatments of transactions and events.

3.2 The concept

✓ Differences viewed from "balance sheet" perspective (IAS 12) are the same as "income statement" approach.

4 ACCOUNTING

4.1 Principle

✓ A deferred tax liability (asset) should be recognised in the statement of financial position.

4.2 Calculation of liability/asset

✓ A comparison of carrying amount and tax bases:

> ➤ Carrying amount > tax base
> ⇒ Taxable temporary difference

> ➤ Carrying amount < tax base
> ⇒ Deductible temporary difference

✓ Generally, deferred tax is provided on **all** temporary differences.

Temporary differences

✓ Usually lead to deferred tax credit (i.e. liability).

✓ Mostly due to income/expense recognition in different periods for accounting profit and taxable profit:

> ➤ accrual basis ≠ cash basis;

> ➤ accounting depreciation ≠ tax allowable depreciation;

> ➤ finance lease treatment (IAS 17) ≠ tax treatment.

Exclusions

✓ Taxable differences do not arise:

> ➤ on expense accruals for tax-disallowed items (e.g. fines);

> ➤ if economic benefits of an asset are not taxable.

✓ To exclude: tax base = carrying amount.

5 DETAILED RULES

5.1 Deferred tax liabilities

✓ Recognise on all taxable temporary differences excluding that which arises from *initial recognition* of:

> ➤ goodwill;

> ➤ assets or liabilities arising in a transaction that:

>> — is not a business combination; and
>> — affects neither profit nor loss.

> For example, initial recognition of a loan (granted or received). Tax base = carrying amount.

✓ Asset revaluation (increases carrying amount) also ⇒ difference if not included in tax base.

5.2　Deferred tax assets

✓　Carrying amount must be:

　➢　reviewed annually;

　➢　reduced to the extent that recovery is not probable.

5.3　Movement on deferred tax

✓　Recognise in profit or loss except:

　➢　on items in other comprehensive income (e.g. revaluation surplus); and

　➢　that arising on business acquisition (is reflected in goodwill).

5.4　Tax rate

✓　Expected to apply when the liability/asset is settled/ realised.

✓　Enacted by the end of the reporting period.

5.5　Exam approach

✓　Set out assets and liabilities carrying amounts and tax bases.

✓　Calculate temporary differences.

✓　Apply tax rate $\Rightarrow$ liability/asset.

✓　Use proforma

	Carrying amount	*Tax base*	*Temporary difference*	*@x%*
Assets	X　–	X	= X/(X)	X
Liabilities	X　–	X	= X/(X)	X

✓　Account for movement in liability:

At start of year	X
To revaluation reserve	X
To profit or loss (balancing figure)	X
Liability at end of year	X

1 DEFINITIONS

Financial instrument – a contract that gives rise to both a financial asset of one entity and a financial liability or equity instrument of another.

1.1 IAS 32

✓ **Financial asset** – any asset that is:

> Cash;

> A contractual right:

– to receive cash (or financial asset);

– to exchange financial instruments under potentially *favourable* conditions;

> an equity instrument of another entity.

✓ **Financial liability** – a contractual obligation to:

> Deliver cash (or other financial asset); or

> Exchange financial instruments under potentially *unfavourable* conditions.

✓ **Equity instrument** – a contract which evidences a residual interest in assets net of liabilities.

1.2 IFRS 9

✓ **Derivative** – a financial instrument which;

> changes value with change in "underlying";

> requires little or no initial net investment; and

> is settled at a future date.

✓ **Amortised cost**:

> initial amount (on recognition);

> minus: principal repayments;

> plus or minus: cumulative amortisation of initial amount less maturity amount (if any difference);

> minus: any impairment write-down.

✓ **Transaction costs** –incremental and directly attributable.

2 PRESENTATION

2.1 Liabilities and equity

✓ **Classify** as liability or equity according to definitions and **substance** on **initial recognition**.

2.2 Settlement in own equity instruments

✓ Does not necessarily result in an equity instrument (definitions apply).

2.3 Offset

✓ Is required if:

> ➢ legal right of offset;
> ➢ settlement on a net basis or simultaneous.

2.4 Compound instruments

✓ Separate presentation of liability and equity components.

✓ Carrying amount of equity component is residual after deduction of liability.

3 RECOGNITION

3.1 Initial recognition

✓ In the statement of financial position on recognition of contractual rights and obligations (includes derivatives).

Initial classification of financial assets

✓ Fair value through profit or loss; or
✓ Fair value through other comprehensive income*; or
✓ Amortised cost*.

* Only these classifications are subject to impairment testing.

3.2 Examples

✓ A forward contract
✓ Financial options
✘ **Not** planned future transactions.

4 FINANCIAL ASSETS

4.1 Initial measurement

All financial assets (except trade receivables) are measured at **fair value**.

✓ Trade receivables at transaction price (IFRS 15).

4.2 Subsequent measurement

✓ Determined by initial classification based on

> ➢ business model; and
> ➢ contractual cash flows.

Classification and measurement summary

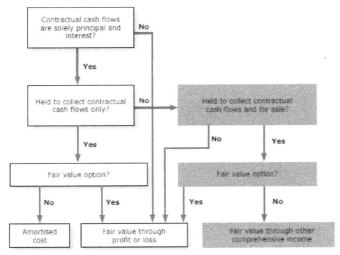

4.3 Amortised cost

✓ Revenue interest is credited to profit or loss.

✓ Carrying amount is increased by any difference between interest revenue and cash received.

4.4 Gains and losses

✓ **Exceptions** to recognition in profit or loss:

➤ hedging relationship;

➤ through other comprehensive income classification.

4.5 Reclassification

✓ Change in business model:

➤ reclassification is **prospective**;

➤ **no** restatement.

5 IMPAIRMENT

5.1 Definitions

✓ **Past due** – contractually due payment not made.

✓ **Credit loss** – present value of all cash shortfalls.

✓ **Lifetime** expected credit losses – arise from all possible default events over expected life of financial asset.

✓ **Loss allowance** – for expected credit losses on:

➤ financial assets subject to impairment testing;

➤ lease receivables;

➤ contract assets (IFRS 15), loan commitments and financial guarantee contracts.

5.2 Loss allowance

✓ Must be recognised in profit or loss.

✓ Measured at each reporting date:

> ➤ **Significant** increase in credit risk ⇒ lifetime expected credit losses;

> ➤ Otherwise 12-month expected credit losses.

5.3 Credit risk

✓ **Probability** of significant increase in credit risk is higher if initial credit risk assessment is low.

✓ Factors that may significantly increase credit risk:

> ➤ Deterioration in the economic environment;
> ➤ Close to breaching covenants;
> ➤ Falling price of debtor's bonds (debt);
> ➤ Fair value < amortised cost;
> ➤ Increase in internal risk grading;
> ➤ Decline in debtor's operating results.

✓ **Rebuttable presumption** > 30 days past due ⇒ recognition of lifetime expected credit losses.

5.4 Trade receivables

✓ Simplified impairment approach – based on lifetime expected credit losses.

✓ Provision matrix – based on:

> ➤ percentages;
> ➤ number of days due past.

6 FINANCIAL LIABILITIES

6.1 Initial recognition

✓ At fair value less transaction costs (expensed to profit or loss).

6.2 Subsequent measurement

✓ Mostly – at amortised cost

✓ Not at amortised cost include:

> ➤ fair value through profit or loss;
> ➤ below-market interest rate loans.

7 DERECOGNITION

7.1 Financial asset

✓ When contractual rights expire or are transferred.

✓ Profit or loss – difference between carrying amount and consideration adjusted for any new asset/liability.

7.2 Financial liability

✓ When contractual rights are extinguished.

✓ Renegotiation at substantially different terms
$\Rightarrow$ derecognition (and recognition of new liability).

8 DISCLOSURE (IFRS 7)

✓ Financial risk management policies:

➢ interest rate risk;
➢ credit risk.

✓ Other:

➢ material items;
➢ carrying amounts pledged as security;
➢ reason for reclassification at amortised cost;
➢ nature and amount of impairment losses.

1 DEFINITIONS

✓ **Business combination** – acquisition of control of another business.

✓ **Acquisition date** – date control acquired.

✓ **Control** – rights to variable returns and ability to affect them through exercise of power.

✓ **Subsidiary** – entity controlled by a **parent**.

✓ **Consolidated financial statements** – present position and performance of a group as a single economic entity.

✓ **Non-controlling interest** – equity in a subsidiary which is not attributable to a parent.

✓ **Goodwill** – an asset representing the future economic benefits not otherwise recognised on acquisition.

2 PARENT AND CONTROL

2.1 Inclusions

✓ All subsidiaries except those excluded by IFRS 10.

Power

✓ Rights to direct activities which affect returns.

✓ Typically holding > 50% voting rights.

✓ Contractual arrangement without majority voting rights.

✓ Can exist even if another has significant influence.

✓ Right can be affect composition of the board directors.

Variable returns

✓ Returns, dividends and profits depend on subsidiary's performance.

✗ **No** fixed right to a specific return.

Link between power and returns

✓ Control = Ability to use *power* to affect *variable returns*

2.2 Exclusions

✓ **ONLY** exclusion is a subsidiary acquired **exclusively** for resale:

➤ IFRS 5 criteria for a disposal group must be met **on acquisition;**

➤ carried at fair value less costs to sell and disclosed separately.

2.3 Exemption from preparation of group accounts

✓ If parent meets all the following criteria:

➤ is a wholly-owned subsidiary (or is partially-owned with consent of non-controlling interest);

➤ does not have publicly traded debt or equity;

➤ does not file financial statements with a recognised stock market;

➤ has own parent which presents consolidated IFRS financial statements.

2.4 Accounting for subsidiaries

Separate financial statements (IAS 27)

✓ In parent's own financial statements:

➤ investments are carried at:

— cost; or

— fair value (under IFRS 9).

➤ dividends are included in profit or loss when right to receive.

2.5 Acquisition method

✓ The **only** method (IFRS 3):

➤ determine acquisition date;

➤ recognise and measure:

— identifiable assets acquired;

— liabilities assumed;

— any non-controlling interest;

— goodwill (or gain from a bargain purchase).

3 SUNDRY PROVISION (IFRS 10)

➤ In consolidated FS

✓ **Eliminate intra-group** transactions, balances and unrealised profit.

✓ Use **same accounting date** or:

➤ prepare subsidiary's at group date; or

➤ use different date not more than 3 months and adjust for significant items.

✓ Must use **uniform accounting policies**.

✓ **Date** of acquisition (disposal) – when *control* passes.

1 THE ISSUE

✓ Separate financial statements are inadequate.

✓ Therefore prepare **consolidated** financial statements in **addition** to separate financial statements.

2 CONCEPTUAL BACKGROUND

2.1 Substance

✓ Replace **cost of investment** with what it represents:

➢ net assets of subsidiary;
➢ carrying amount of goodwill.

✓ Adjust for non-controlling interest.

✓ Credit consolidated reserves with parent's share of subsidiary's post-acquisition profit.

2.2 Goodwill

Consideration*	X
Non-controlling interest*	X
Less: Identifiable net assets*	(X)
Goodwill at acquisition	X

* All at fair value.

3 OVERVIEW OF TECHNIQUE

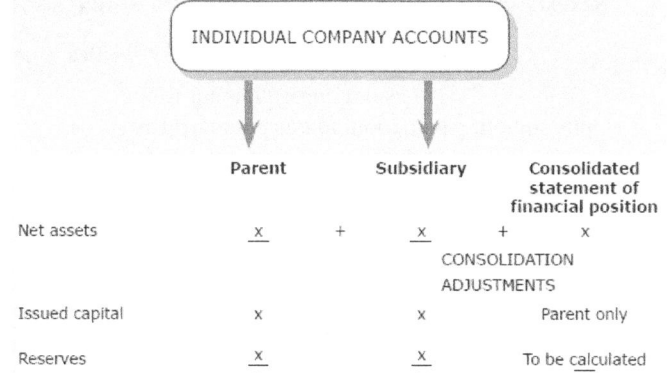

3.1 Individual company accounts

✓ Finalise in accordance with IFRS *before* consolidation.

3.2 Consolidation adjustments

✓ Major adjustments:

➢ Goodwill;
➢ Non-controlling interests;
➢ Consolidated reserves.

4 CONSOLIDATED STATEMENT OF FINANCIAL POSITION

4.1 Goodwill

✓ Recognise as an asset on acquisition.

✓ Test annually for impairment (IFRS 3).

4.2 Post-acquisition growth in reserves

✓ Include parent's share of subsidiary's post-acquisition profit/(loss) in consolidated retained earnings.

4.3 Non-controlling interest

✓ Net assets not owned by the parent measured at:

  ➢ proportionate share of identifiable net assets (i.e. *without* goodwill); or
  ➢ fair value (i.e. *with* share of goodwill).

✓ Presented as a *separate* component of equity.

EXAM APPROACH

✓ Establish group structure.

✓ Set up pro-forma net asset statement.

✓ Work through question adjusting statement of financial position, net asset schedule and consolidated retained earnings (CRE):

➢ Unrealised profits;
➢ Intra-group balances and items in transit;
➢ Items not yet accounted for;
➢ Fair value adjustments;
➢ Group accounting policy adjustments.

✓ Finish net assets schedule

✓ Calculate goodwill

➢ Cost of investment;
➢ Plus value of non-controlling interest (NCI);
➢ Less subsidiary's net assets at acquisition;
➢ Impaired – to CRE and NCI (if included);
➢ Remaining – to consolidated statement of financial position.

✓ Calculate NCI

➢ Value on acquisition;
➢ Plus % of post-acquisition profits;
➢ Less share of goodwill impairment (if applicable).

✓ Calculate CRE

➢ All of parent;
➢ Parent's % of subsidiary's post-acquisition profits;
➢ Less impaired goodwill;
➢ Add across and down.

1   MID-YEAR ACQUISITIONS

✓   Calculate subsidiary's net assets at date of acquisition.

✓   Assume profit after tax accrues evenly over time – **unless** told otherwise.

2   INTRA-GROUP TRADING

2.1   Balances

✓   Typically recorded in "current accounts".

✓   Must be eliminated on consolidation.

✓   Intra-group transactions (income and expenses) must be eliminated from consolidated profit or loss and other comprehensive income. "Direction" of transaction is **irrelevant**.

2.2   Unrealised profit

✓   Adjustment is necessary if inventory remains unsold from *group* perspective:

Dr   Profit of selling company* $x
      Cr   Inventory $x

* Adjust consolidated retained earnings of parent *or* net assets of subsidiary.

2.3   Inventory

✓   At the lower of cost and net realisable value to the *group*.

2.4   Non-current asset transfers

✓   Account for at the amount as if the transfer had not been made.

✓   On consolidation, eliminate any gain/loss on "disposal".

✓   Adjust depreciation charge:

➤   as individual company adjustment; or
➤   on consolidation.

1 ADJUSTMENTS

✓ Consolidation problems are usually tackled in two stages:

    (1)   Process any individual company adjustments;

    (2)   Do the consolidation.

2 ITEMS NOT ACCOUNTED FOR

2.1 Updating accounts

✓ Financial statements of individual entities must be complete and correct *before* consolidation.

2.2 Dividends payable

✓ Account for *before* consolidation:

In subsidiary's books

Dr	Equity	$x	
	Cr Current liability		$x

In parent's books (its share)

Dr	Dividend receivable	$x	
	Cr Profit or loss		$x

✓ Cancel intra-group liability on consolidation.

2.3 Partially recorded dividends

! Read the question.

2.4 Dividends paid out of pre-acquisition profits

✓ Include in parent's profit or loss.

3 ACCOUNTING POLICY ADJUSTMENTS

3.1 Group policy

✓ Adjustment may be needed if subsidiary:

    ➤   acquired mid-year;

    ➤   prepares accounts under local GAAP.

3.2 Investment property

✓ Account for from *group* perspective (i.e. under IAS 16 if owner-occupied).

4 GOODWILL

4.1 Definition

✓ An asset representing the future economic benefits not otherwise recognised on acquisition:

Consideration*	X
Non-controlling interest*	X
Less: Identifiable net assets*	(X)
Goodwill at acquisition	X

* All at fair value.

✓ Non-controlling interest may be measured directly or indirectly (e.g. number of shares × market price).

4.2 Fair value of purchase consideration

✘ **Excludes** direct costs of acquisition:

  ➢ must expense to profit or loss;
  ➢ reduces amount of goodwill recognised.

Deferred consideration

✓ **Discount** to present value.

Contingent consideration

✓ If payable in cash: Cr Liability
✓ If to be settled in shares: Cr Equity

Share exchange

✓ Multiplying the number of shares issued by the market price at the date of acquisition.

4.3 Recognition

Identifiable net assets

✓ Some assets (e.g. intangibles) **not** recognised in the subsidiary's statement of financial position **will** be recognised in the consolidated financial statements.

✓ A subsidiary's contingent liabilities are recognised if fair value can be measured reliably (IFRS 3).

4.4 Measurement

Non-controlling interest

✓ Either:

  ➢ fair value; or
  ➢ proportionate share of the subsidiary's identifiable net assets.

⌐ Can choose for **each** acquisition.

4.5 Fair values

✓ Per IFRS 13 must reflect "highest and best use".

5 FAIR VALUE ADJUSTMENTS

5.1 Exam complication

- ✓ "Fair value exercise" (IFRS 3) is **not** revaluation per IAS 16.

- ✓ Any changes in fair value post-acquisition must be adjusted against consolidated retained earnings.

Depreciating assets

- ✓ "Depreciate" fair value difference.

Non-depreciating assets (land)

- ✓ No adjustment required.

Inventory

- ✓ Fair value difference remains to the extent that goods have not been sold.

Contingent liabilities

- ✓ Adjust net assets for any post-acquisition change in fair value.

5.2 Accounting for the adjustment

- ✓ Reflect entire fair value difference in consolidate financial statements.

- ✓ Non-controlling interest share in difference and any consequential depreciation adjustment.

5.3 Post-acquisition changes in subsidiary's reserves

- ✓ Include parent's share in consolidated retained earnings.

- ✓ Non-controlling interest's share is included in non-controlling interest.

6 ACCOUNTING FOR GOODWILL

6.1 Recognition and measurement

- ✓ Initially – at cost (which is a fair value) in accordance with IFRS 3.

- ✓ Subsequently – at cost less impairment losses.

☞ Goodwill must be tested **annually** for impairment.

6.2 Bargain purchase ("excess")

✓ If an excess still remains after reassessment it is recognised **immediately** in profit or loss.

✓ Factors that may give rise to excess:

➤ future costs not recognised;
➤ measurement of items not at fair value;
➤ genuine "bargain".

6.3 Initial accounting determined provisionally

Provisional accounting

✓ Adjustment is **retrospective** during the "measurement period".

⚷ This is an **exception** to the normal rule in IAS 8.

Measurement period

✓ **Maximum one year** after acquisition date.

Adjustments after measurement period

✓ In accordance with IAS 8.

6.4 Impairment

✓ Goodwill must be allocated to a CGU (usually, but not necessarily, the subsidiary).

⚷ Goodwill must be "gross" of any non-controlling interest's share for impairment testing purposes.

✓ "Grossing-up" is only necessary if non-controlling interest is measured at proportionate share of identifiable net assets.

1 CONCEPT

✓ Same principle as statement of financial position:

➢ determine profits generated by assets under the control of parent;

➢ then deduct what is owned by non-controlling interest).

✓ Effect is to replace dividend income with parent's % of the subsidiary's profit after tax.

✓ Eliminate intra-group transactions (single-entity concept).

2 INTRA-GROUP TRANSACTIONS

2.1 Dividends

✓ Cancel parent's income against subsidiary's dividends paid and payable.

✓ Since non-controlling interest is based on profit it automatically includes its share of any appropriation (i.e. dividend) – so no adjustment required.

✓ Dividend income in consolidated statement of profit or loss is from **trade investments** only.

2.2 Other intra-group items

Trading

✓ Deduct intra-group revenue from revenue and cost of sales.

Unrealised profit in closing inventory

✓ Adjust against profit of selling company:

➢ consolidated retained earnings of parent; *or*
➢ net assets of subsidiary.

Unrealised profit in opening inventory

✓ As for closing inventory but **cannot** affect inventory in statement of financial position.

Non-current asset transfers

✓ Consolidated statement of profit or loss:

➢ **includes** deprecation based on cost to the group;
➢ **excludes** any gain/loss on transfer (it is unrealised).

Interest and other charges (e.g. management charge)

✓ Eliminate income and expense.

3 NON-CONTROLLING INTEREST

3.1 Recognition

✓ Profit after tax attributable to non-controlling interest must be disclosed separately (IAS 1).

3.2 Goodwill

✓ Any impairment must be shared between parent and non-controlling interest (if measured at fair value).

4 MID-YEAR ACQUISITIONS

4.1 Inclusion of subsidiary's results

✓ From acquisition date.

✓ Assume revenue and expenses accrue evenly over time.

EXAM APPROACH

✓ Establish group structure.

✓ Set up pro-forma statement – parent + subsidiary

✓ Work through question:

➢ Sum each line item from revenue down to profit after tax, *unless* mid-year acquisition (in which case time apportion subsidiary);

➢ Profit attributable to NCI is % × subsidiary's profit after tax;

➢ Dividend income – from trade investments only;

✓ Dividend appropriation (in statement of changes in equity) – parent's dividends only.

1 EQUITY ACCOUNTING

1.1 Nature of relationship

✓ Used to reflect an interest in net assets and results of a company which is:

➢ more than a passive interest in a trade investment;
➢ less than a controlling interest.

1.2 Scope

✓ IAS 28 also includes accounting for joint ventures – but these are **not examinable** at F7.

1.3 Definitions

✓ **Associate** – an entity over which an investor has significant influence.

✓ **Significant influence** – power to participate in financial and operation policy decisions but not control.

✓ **Equity method** of accounting for investments:

➢ initial recognition at cost;
➢ adjusted for post-acquisition share of net assets;
➢ profit or loss and other comprehensive income each include share.

1.4 Significant influence

✓ May be evidenced by:

➢ Board representation;
➢ Participation in policy-making';
➢ Material inter-company transactions;
➢ Inter-change of managerial personnel;
➢ Provision of essential technical information.

✓ Presumed if voting rights $\geq 20\%$.

✓ If significant influence is lost carrying amount (under IAS 28) becomes cost (for IFRS 9).

1.5 Separate financial statements

✓ Investors who are exempt from the requirement to equity account (see §2.8) may present separate financial statements as their only financial statements.

✓ In separate financial statements, an associate should be accounted for:

➢ under IFRS 5 if classified as held for sale;
➢ at cost or in accordance with IFRS 9.

2   ACCOUNTING TREATMENT

2.1   Relationship to a group

✖ An associate is **not** part of a group.

2.2   Basic rule

🔑 The equity method is the **only** method of accounting for an investment in an associate.

✓ Rule applies unless investor is exempt from equity accounting requirement (see §2.8).

2.3   Equity accounting

✖ Is **not** consolidation (i.e. on a line by line basis).

✓ Increase/decrease **cost of investment** by investor's % of associate's post-acquisition profits or losses.

> ➤ Carrying amount is *single* line item;
> ➤ Already includes goodwill;
> ➤ Dividends received reduce carrying amount.

✓ Other side of entry is profit or loss (and other comprehensive income, if relevant).

2.4   In financial statements

In statement of financial position

Cost of investment	X
% share of post-acquisition profits	X
Less: Goodwill impaired	(X)
Carrying amount	X

In profit or loss and other comprehensive income

✓ Separate line items for investor's share of:

> ➤ profit after tax (replaces dividend income); and
> ➤ other comprehensive income (if any).

✓ Time-apportion if mid-year acquisition.

2.5   Accounting policies

✓ May differ (by definition as associate is not controlled).

✓ Adjust on equity accounting.

2.6 Year ends

✓ Use associate's most recent financial statements.

✓ If not coterminous:

➢ prepare additional financial statements; or
➢ make adjustments.

✓ Difference should not exceed 3 months.

2.7 Impairment

✓ Recognition – in accordance with IFRS 9.

✓ Measurement – in accordance with IAS 36.

✓ Test carrying amount of investment (not goodwill).

2.8 Exemptions to equity accounting

✓ Two main exemptions are:

➢ Classified as held-for-sale (IFRS 5);
➢ Investor is a parent which meets the criteria that exempt it from preparing group accounts.

3 IN CONSOLIDATED FINANCIAL STATEMENTS

3.1 Inter-company trading

✗ **No** elimination or adjustment.

✓ Show amounts due from/to associates as separate receivables/payables.

3.2 Dividends

✓ Consolidated statement of financial position will include amount receivable by the group.

✗ **Not** included in profit or loss.

━ Dividend is a distribution of profit already included under equity method.

3.3 Unrealised profit

✓ Eliminate investor's interest by deducting from associate's profit before tax and retained earnings.

1 GENERAL PURPOSE FINANCIAL STATEMENTS

✓ Provide information for external users:

> - investors;
> - employees;
> - lenders;
> - suppliers and other creditors;
> - customers;
> - governments and agencies;
> - public.

✓ Not all organisations are concerned with profit.

2 INTERPRETATION OF ACCOUNTS

2.1 Summary

✓ Involves:

> - Identifying users.;
> - Examining financial information;
> - Analysis (comparison, evaluation and prediction);
> - Reporting (information for economic decision-making).

Users' requirements

✓ Internal:

> - To improve competitive standing;
> - To identify opportunities to improve performance.

✓ External – generally have access only to published financial statements.

2.2 Use of ratios

✓ To assist analysis by focussing on:

> - patterns over time ("trend analysis");
> - weakness (areas for further investigation).

Typical comparisons

✓ Historical (current against previous periods).

✓ Against market information (other companies/industry averages, etc).

✓ Actual against targets/budgets/standards.

2.3 Influences on ratios

Business factors

✓ Type of business.
✓ Quality of management.
✓ State of economy and market conditions.
✓ Management actions.
✓ Changes in the business.
✓ Transactions not "at arm's length".

Accounting policies

- ✓ Depreciation:

    - ➢ in full in year of acquisition?
    - ➢ straight-line or reducing balance?
    - ➢ estimated useful life?
    - ➢ residual value?

- ✓ IAS 16 revaluation *v* cost model.

- ✓ IAS 2 FIFO *v* weighted average.

2.4 Limitations

- ✖ Analysis is essentially retrospective.
- ✖ Based on accounting rather than economic data.
- ✖ Limitations of financial statements
- ✖ Different accounting policies.
- ✖ Reliability of industry statistics.
- ✖ Loss of detailed information and extremes.
- ✖ Difficulties in making comparisons.
- ✖ Ratios at a point in time may be unrepresentative.

2.5 Other sources of information for analysis

- ✓ Absolute comparisons.

- ✓ Background information about nature of business.

- ✓ Statement of cash flows.

- ✓ Non-financial indicators, for example:

    - ➢ staff turnover;
    - ➢ productivity;
    - ➢ compliance;
    - ➢ customer satisfaction.

2.6 Creative accounting

- ✓ Off-balance sheet financing – unrecorded liabilities.

- ✓ Profit manipulation/smoothing.

- ✓ Window dressing (e.g. through incorrect "cut-off" at reporting date).

3 ACCOUNTING RATIOS

Main areas

- ✓ Performance

- ✓ Liquidity:

    - ➢ Short-term;
    - ➢ Long-term.

- ✓ Efficiency

- ✓ Investors.

4 PERFORMANCE

4.1 Significance

✓ Used to assess how well management uses resources.

4.2 Key ratios

Return on capital employed (ROCE)

✓ $\dfrac{\text{Profit before interest and tax}}{\text{Capital employed}} \times 100$

✓ Capital employed:

➢ share capital + reserves + long-term liabilities;
= *total* assets less *current* liabilities;
➢ may be year-end or average.

✓ A measure of overall efficiency.

Return on shareholders' funds (Return on equity)

✓ $\dfrac{\text{Profit before tax}}{\text{Share capital} + \text{reserves}} \times 100$

✓ A measure of efficiency of use of funds provided by shareholders.

Gross profit %

✓ $\dfrac{\text{Gross profit}}{\text{Revenue}} \times 100$

✓ Margin earned on sales.

4.3 Analysis

✓ Low/falling ROCE may indicate:

➢ inefficient use of resources;
➢ a future loss if economy deteriorate;
➢ need to increase operating profit;
➢ need to sell some assets and invest proceeds for a higher return.

🔑 ROCE should **exceed cost of any borrowing**.

✓ Can be analysed as $= \dfrac{\text{Profit}}{\text{Revenue}} \times \dfrac{\text{Revenue}}{\text{Capital employed}}$

➢ Profit margin is *qualitative* measure of profit;
➢ Asset turnover is a *quantitative* measure of use.

5 LIQUIDITY

5.1 Short-term

Significance

✓ Ability to raise cash to meet payment obligations.

✓ Statement of cash flows may be more useful.

Key ratios

✓ **Current** ratio $= \dfrac{\text{Current assets}}{\text{Current liabilities}}$

✓ A measure of adequacy of current assets to meet short-term liabilities (without having to raise more finance).

✓ Quick ratio $= \dfrac{\text{Current assets} - \text{inventory}}{\text{Current liabilities}}$

✓ A measure of real (more immediate) solvency.

✓ Higher ratios are normally preferable (more liquid).

! Low/falling ratios may indicate:

   ✗ **overtrading**;

   ✗ doubts about **going concern**;

   ✗ undercapitalisation.

Overtrading – rapid increase in turnover without secure additional long-term capital (i.e. **under**capitalised).

! High/increasing ratio may indicate:

   ✗ **undertrading** or **overcapitalisation**;

   ✗ **over-investment** in current assets.

✓ If going concern in doubt compare operating overdraft with limit of facility (if information available.)

"Window-dressing"

A form of creating accounting used to present financial statements in a more favourable light.

"Uses"

✓ To obtain funds/borrow money.
✓ To reduce tax payments.
✓ To "smooth" profits.
✓ To hide liquidity/profitability problems due to poor management decisions.

5.2 Long-term

Significance

✓ Examine the financing structure.
✓ Indicate risks to providers of capital.

Gearing ratio ("leverage")

✓ $\dfrac{\text{Debt}}{\text{Equity}}$ (more sensitive);or

✓ $\dfrac{\text{Debt}}{\text{Debt + equity}}$

  ➢ Debt includes long-term loans, preferred shares and "permanent" overdrafts.

  ➢ Equity is "residual" (ordinary shares and reserves).

✓ Borrowings (for fixed return) to equity is an indicator of financial risk (the risk of insolvency).

✓ High gearing suits entities with:

  ➢ stable profits (to meet interest payments); and
  ➢ suitable asset backing for security (e.g. property).

Interest cover

✓ $\dfrac{\text{Profit before interest}}{\text{Interest}}$

✓ Indicates ability to meet interest expense out of profits.

✗ Ratio < 2 is usually considered unsatisfactory.

✓ Interest must be paid first, even if profits fall.

! Low/falling ratio may indicate:

  ✗ potential difficulty financing debts if profits fall;
  ✗ doubts about **going concern**;
  ✗ increased risk to shareholders of falling dividends.

6 EFFICIENCY

6.1 Significance

✓ Working capital ratios show management's effectiveness in running the business efficiently.

✓ For a given level of activity profitability is maximised when working capital is minimised.

6.2 Key ratios

Inventory turnover

✓ As no. of times = $\dfrac{\text{Cost of sales}}{\text{Inventories}^{1}}$

✓ Inventory days = $\dfrac{\text{Inventories}^{1}}{\text{Cost of sales}} \times 365$

✓ Inventory may be:

  ➢ closing (highlights effect of major changes); or
  ➢ average (has "dampening" effect).

✓ A measure of operational and marketing efficiency.

✓ High/increasing turnover (i.e. low/decreasing days) generally indicates efficiency in selling.

Receivable days ("collection period")

✓ $\dfrac{\text{Average trade receivables}}{\text{Credit sales}} \times 365$

Shows (average) time (no. of days) credit customers take to pay.

✓ If days ↑ the expense of collecting debts ↑. May be due to:

> ➢ weak credit control;
> ➢ policy to extend more credit;
> ➢ different credit terms (e.g. for major customers).

Payable days ("average payment period")

✓ $\dfrac{\text{Average trade payables}}{\text{Credit purchases}} \times 365$

✓ Shows (average) no. of days taken to pay suppliers.

✓ Days ↑ may be due to liquidity problems:

> ➢ poor reputation;
> ➢ withdrawal of credit and/or supplies;
> ➢ loss of cash discounts/penalty payments.

✓ Can be deliberate to take advantage of interest free credit.

6.3 Working capital (cash conversion) cycle

✓ No. of days = Inventory days + receivable days – payable days.

✓ Can be negative (e.g. a supermarket) if cash received before paying suppliers.

✓ Shows amount of working capital needed to operate.

✓ It is the difference between current assets and current liabilities.

✓ If cycle ↑ may be due to:

> ➢ poor working capital control;
> ➢ deliberate policy (e.g. to hold more goods/extend credit to customers).

7 INVESTORS' RATIOS

7.1 Significance

✓ Establish characteristics:

> ➢ EPS – is important for capital growth;
> ➢ Dividends – are important for income generation.

✓ Dividend yield $= \dfrac{\text{Dividend per share}}{\text{Current market price per share}}$

✓ Dividend cover $= \dfrac{\text{Earnings per share (EPS)}}{\text{Dividend per share}}$

✓ Price/earnings (P/E) ratio

$= \dfrac{\text{Current market price per share}}{\text{EPS}}$

✓ See section 27 for EPS.

8 EXAM TECHNIQUE

8.1 Which formula?

☞ Calculate only what the information given will allow.

✓ State formula used.
✓ If no comparative information use closing balances.
✓ Use cost of goods as an approximation to credit purchases.

8.2 If asked to interpret

✓ Calculate only what you can use.

✓ Make concise comments relevant to *audience*:

> ➢ What does the ratio mean/show?
> ➢ What does a change mean/show?
> ➢ What is the norm (if relevant)?
> ➢ How might the change have arisen?
> ➢ What is the significance of ↑/↓ for future (i.e. implications)?

✓ Take an overview (i.e. summarise the whole picture).

1 CASH FLOWS

1.1 Scope of IAS 7

✓ All entities.
✓ A separate statement.

1.2 Benefits

✓ Provides information to users to evaluate changes in:

> net assets;
> financial structure;
> ability to affect amounts and timing of cash flows.

✓ Helps assess ability to generate cash/cash equivalents.

✓ Useful in comparing different entities.

✓ Cash is cash – eliminates effects of alternative accounting bases.

✓ Historical cash flow information may indicate future cash flows.

✓ Focus on cash management can improve results.

1.3 Definitions

✓ *Cash* – cash on hand and demand deposits.

✓ *Cash equivalents* – short-term, highly liquid investments.

✓ *Cash flows* – inflows and outflows of cash and cash equivalents.

2 PRESENTATION

2.1 Classification

✓ **Operating** – principal revenue-producing activities.

✓ **Investing** – acquisition and disposal of long-term assets, etc.

✓ **Financing** – change amount and composition of equity capital and borrowings.

3 OPERATING ACTIVITIES

3.1 Direct method (encouraged)

Show major classes of gross cash receipts/payments:

✓ directly from *accounting records*; or

✓ by adjusting sales/cost of sales:

> changes in inventories/receivables/payables;
> other non-cash items;
> cash effects which are investing/financing.

Technique

Step 1   Cash receipts (from customers)
            Less: Cash paid (to suppliers/employees)

            $\Rightarrow$ Cash generated from operations.

Step 2   Payments for interest and income taxes.

            $\Rightarrow$ Net cash from operating activities.

3.2   Indirect method

Adjusts *profit or loss* for effects of:

✓   non-cash transactions (e.g. depreciation);

✓   deferrals/accruals of past/future operating cash receipts/ payments;

✓   items of income/expense relating to investing/ financing cash flows.

Technique

Step 1(a)   Start with profit before tax.

Step 1(b)   Adjust for:

               ✓   non-cash items; and
               ✓   investing/financing items on accruals basis (e.g. interest).

               $\Rightarrow$ Operating profit before working capital changes.

Step 1(c)   Make working capital changes.

               $\Rightarrow$ Cash generated from operations (same figure as for direct method)

Step 2   As for direct method.

2602

3.3 Proformas

Indirect method

Cash flows from operating activities

	$	$
Profit before taxation	x	
Adjustments for:		
Depreciation [1]	x	
Investment income	(x)	
Interest expense	x	
Operating profit before working capital changes	x	
Increase in trade and other receivables	(x)	
Decrease in inventories	x	
Decrease in trade payables	(x)	
Cash generated from operations	x	
Interest paid	(x)	
Income taxes paid	(x)	

Net cash from operating activities   x

Cash flows from investing activities

Purchase of property, plant and equipment	(x)	
Proceeds from sale of equipment	x	
Interest received	x	
Dividends received	x	

Net cash used in investing activities   x

Continued $ $

Cash flows from financing activities

Proceeds from issuance of share capital	x	
Proceeds from long-term borrowings	x	
Dividends paid	(x)	

Net cash used in financing activities   x

Net increase in cash and cash equivalents   x
Cash and cash equivalents at beginning of period   x

Cash and cash equivalents at end of period   x

Direct method

Cash flows from operating activities

Cash receipts from customers	x	
Cash paid to suppliers and employees	(x)	

Cash generated from operations	x	

...remainder as for the indirect method

[1] Similarly losses/(gains) on non-current asset disposals.

Exam tips!

✓ Start answer at the bottom (opening and closing cash and cash equivalents) – the difference (change in year) is the amount to be reconciled.

✓ Return to top – profit *before* tax is the starting point.

3.4 Which method?

Direct method

✓ Better fulfils information needs of users.

✗ Many entities do not collect information to facilitate this method.

✗ Net cash flow from operations is not a better measure of performance than profit.

✗ Requires supplementary disclosure.

Indirect method

✓ Focuses on difference between profit and net cash flow from operations.

✓ Provides "linkage" to other financial statements.

4 CASH FLOW ANALYSIS

✓ Have cash and cash equivalents increased or decreased?

✓ Operating cash flows:

➢ Evidence of overtrading?
➢ Interest expense *v* interest paid.

✓ Investing cash flows:

➢ Depreciation *v* purchase of non-current assets.
➢ How are new assets financed?
➢ Profit or loss on sale of non-current assets?

✓ Financing cash flows:

➢ Debt *v* equity.
➢ Dividend payments.

5 DISCLOSURES

✓ Reconciliation of cash and cash equivalents.

✓ Major non-cash transactions:

➢ issue of shares to acquire assets;
➢ conversion of debt to equity; and
➢ lease arrangements.

✓ Voluntary disclosures:

➢ available borrowings – unused and any restrictions;
➢ cash flows that represent increases in capacity.

1   IAS 33

1.1   Earnings performance

✓   EPS shows *trend*.

1.2   Scope

Separate financial statements of entities whose debt or equity instruments are publicly traded.

✓   Also **consolidated** financial statements of such entities.

1.3   Definitions

✓   **Ordinary share** – equity instrument that is subordinate to all other equity instruments.

✓   **Equity instrument** – a contract which evidences a residual interest in entity's net assets.

✓   **Potential ordinary share** – a contract which may entitle its holder to ordinary shares. For example:

➢   convertible instruments;
➢   share options and warrants;
➢   share purchase plans.

✓   **Options, warrants**, etc –give holder the right to purchase ordinary shares.

✓   **Dilution** – reduction in EPS (or increase in loss per share) if rights relating to convertible instruments, options, warrants, etc are exercised.

✓   **Anti-dilution** – opposite effect of dilution.

✓   **Contingently issuable ordinary shares** – ordinary shares issuable for little or no consideration.

2   EARNINGS PER SHARE

2.1   Basic EPS

✓   Presented for profit or loss attributable to ordinary shareholders.

✓   Also for continuing operations (if presented).

$$EPS = \frac{\text{Profit or loss attributable to ordinary equity holders}}{\text{Weighted average number of ordinary shares}}$$

2.2   Which earnings?

✓   As defined above adjusted for:

➢   post-tax effect of preference dividends; and
➢   non-controlling interest.

2701

3 WEIGHTED AVERAGE NUMBER OF SHARES

3.1 Basic rule

✓ Outstanding during the period.

✓ Adjust number in existence at beginning of period for shares issued for (full) consideration during the period:

➢ in cash;
➢ to acquire a controlling interest in another entity; or
➢ to redeem debt.

✓ Weight the number of shares from date of issue.

3.2 Share issues with no cash consideration

✓ Adjust weighted average number (for all periods presented) for:

➢ bonus issues and bonus elements;
➢ share splits and reverse share splits.

Bonus issues

☞ Treat as if new shares issued for whole period.

✓ Multiply number of shares in issue by bonus fraction.

✓ EPS will **fall**.

✓ Adjust comparatives (× by *inverse* of bonus fraction).

Rights issues

✓ Has features in common with bonus issue *and* issue at full market price:

➢ Apply bonus fraction to number of shares in issue before rights issue;

➢ New shares issued are pro-rated as for issues for consideration.

✓ Bonus fraction

$$= \frac{\text{Cum - rights price per share}}{\text{Theoretical ex - rights price per share ("TERP")}}$$

✓ Comparative EPS must be restated for bonus element (× last-years EPS by *inverse* of bonus fraction).

4 DILUTED EPS

4.1 Purpose

✓ A warning to existing shareholders that EPS may fall (e.g. when share options are exercised).

✓ Potential ordinary shares are treated as dilutive **only** if conversion would decrease earnings/increase loss per share *from continuing operations*.

4.2   Convertible instruments

✓   Calculate new EPS using:

➢   a new number of shares;
➢   a new earnings figure.

New number of ordinary shares

✓   Weighted average per basic EPS calculation
+
Weighted average that would be issued on conversion:

➢   Presume maximum number that could be issued;
➢   Deemed converted at beginning of period (or date of issue, if later).

New earnings figure

✓   As per basic EPS adjusted for after-tax effect of conversion, for example:

➢   dividends on dilutive potential ordinary shares deducted;

➢   interest on dilutive potential ordinary shares.

4.3   Options, warrants, etc

✓   Assume exercise of dilutive options:

➢   Assume proceeds at fair value;

➢   Treat the difference between the number of shares issued and the number of shares that would have been issued at fair value as for no consideration.

Options are dilutive if shares are issued at below fair value.

✓   Each issue has two contracts

(1)   to issue a number of shares at a fair value (average for the period) – These are *non-dilutive;*

(2)   to issue the remainder for no consideration (a bonus issue) – These are *dilutive.*

5   SIGNIFICANCE OF EPS

5.1   EPS *v* earnings

✓   A relative measure *v* an actual measure.

✓   EPS allows comparison between different-sized companies.

5.2   Performance measure

✓   Used in the calculation of price/earnings ratio.

5.3 Problems

- ✘ Affected by choice of accounting policies.
- ✘ Based on historical information.
- ✘ High EPS may be "bad" (e.g. due to lack of investment).
- ✘ Only a measure of profitability.

6 PRESENTATION AND DISCLOSURE

6.1 Presentation

- ✓ In the statement other comprehensive income.
- ✓ With equal prominence for *all* periods.

6.2 Disclosure

General

- ✓ Amounts used reconciled to profit or loss for the period.
- ✓ Number of shares reconciled between basic and diluted.
- ✓ Anti-dilutive instruments excluded from dilutive EPS.
- ✓ Significant share transactions after the reporting date.

Additional EPS

- ✓ Use only weighted average number per IAS 33.

- ✓ Additional profit figure must be reconciled to a line item in the statement of comprehensive income.

ARTICLES

The following technical articles written by members of the F7 examining team can be found on the ACCA website at:

http://www.accaglobal.com/uk/en/student/exam-support-resources/fundamentals-exams-study-resources/f7/technical-articles.html

The need for and an understanding of a conceptual framework
IFRS 3 Business Combinations   Member of F7 exam team   SA July 2010

Exam technique

Multiple-choice questions
How to approach performance appraisal questions
Examiner's report to December 2014   *See summary in later section*
The following articles can be found in the following section:

Off Balance Sheet Financing
David Beckham: Asset or liability?

SPECIAL FEATURES

Examiner approach article – see http://www.accaglobal.com/uk/en/student/exam-support-resources/fundamentals-exams-study-resources/f7/technical-articles/examiner-approach.html

Examiner's approach interview – see http://examinerinterviews.accaglobal.com/Channel/Examiner%20Interviews/Approach/F7

See also IASB website = www.iasb.org.uk

✓   IASB Update details subjects discussed at IASB meetings http://www.ifrs.org/Updates/Pages/Updates.aspx

"OFF BALANCE SHEET FINANCING"

This article looks at the importance of including assets and the corresponding liabilities in the statement of financial position. In order to explain why the accounting profession has taken steps to try and eliminate the use of "off balance sheet financing" we will use a simple example.

A company leases an asset with a fair value of $20. We will show the implications on two key ratios of both including and excluding the asset from the statement of financial position.

Firstly we will consider the **legal form** of the transaction, as we have entered into a lease contract we do not legally own the asset and will therefore exclude the asset from the statement of financial position. What is shown below is a simple statement of financial position that excludes the asset.

EQUITY 80	ASSETS 100
DEBT 20	

PROFIT FOR THE YEAR = 20

Given this simple statement of financial position we can calculate two key ratios:

✓   Return on Capital Employed (ROCE)

$$= \frac{\text{Profit}}{\text{Total Capital Employed}}$$

✓ $\text{Gearing} = \dfrac{\text{Debt}}{\text{Debt} + \text{Equity}}$

ROCE $= \dfrac{20}{100} = 20\%$

Gearing $= \dfrac{20}{20 + 80} = 20\%$

We will now consider the **substance** of the transaction, which is that the company has entered into a finance lease and has control of the asset. As the use of the asset is controlled it must now be included in the statement of financial position. By including the asset in the statement of financial position we must balance the "other side" by increasing the amount of debt. The substance of a finance lease is that we have obtained a loan to finance the acquisition of the asset and therefore we must include that liability in the statement of financial position.

2901

EQUITY 80	ASSETS 120
DEBT 40	

PROFIT FOR THE YEAR = 20

To keep the example simple we are saying the profit is still 20. In real life the profit will be reduced as we have an asset that needs depreciating and we have also taken on board a loan which will carry an interest charge. However profits will increase due to the fact that the lease rental will no longer be charged to profit or loss. For the purposes of this example we will assume that the increase and decrease in profits will balance each other out and will still be 20.

Recalculating the key ratios:

$$\text{ROCE} \quad = \frac{20}{120} \quad = 16.7\%$$

$$\text{Gearing} \quad = \frac{40}{40 + 80} \quad = 33.3\%$$

We can now see that by including the asset and corresponding liability in the statement of financial position our key ratios have worsened, ROCE has gone down and gearing, as a measure of risk, has increased.

This example illustrates why companies would prefer to keep assets and liabilities "off balance sheet". The IASB has gone some way to preventing this by issuing accounting standards, such as IAS 17.

However, it is unlikely that "off balance sheet financing" will be fully eradicated because as soon as the IASB closes one "loophole" the preparers off accounts will try some new method of keeping the asset and liability out of the statement of financial position. You only have to look at the news to see that high profile companies are going into liquidation, in some event due to them having employed accounting treatments that kept the asset and liability out of the financial statements.

This article has used an asset acquired using a finance lease to explain the concept of "off balance sheet financing", but it is not the only way that assets and liabilities could be excluded from the statement of financial position.

It is highly likely that this concept of "Off balance sheet financing" will be encountered sometime during your ACCA studies in the financial reporting papers.

DAVID BECKHAM: ASSET OR LIABILITY?

Any of you out there who do not know who David Beckham is? Just to make sure, he is a footballer who used to play for Manchester United and England who is married to Victoria Beckham, ex "Posh Spice" from the Spice Girls. For the purposes of this article I am going to presume that David Beckham is still playing for Manchester United.

Now that we have identified who David Beckham is, what I want to ask you is whether or not Manchester United includes David Beckham as an asset in its statement of financial position. In order to answer that question we need to identify what is an asset. Assets are defined by the IASB in the *Conceptual Framework*.

An asset is defined as:

✓ A resource:

  ➢ Controlled;
  ➢ With ability to generate future economic benefits;
  ➢ As a result of a past transaction.

Does Manchester United control David Beckham? I believe the answer to that question is yes. Manchester and Beckham have signed a contract that David Beckham will play football for United. United can therefore control how Beckham will be used in the best interest of Manchester United.

Will David Beckham generate future economic benefits for Manchester United? Again the answer to this is probable yes. He is a fairly decent footballer who has helped United in their quest for trophies (and therefore money) both in UK and in Europe. He generates a lot of public interest and TV companies are willing to pay United to screen their games. Also there is the merchandising side whereby shirts etc are sold with Beckham's name or endorsement added, which will all have an effect of generating future benefits.

Did Manchester acquire David Beckham as a result of a past transaction? The answer to this question is no. David Beckham was never acquired by Manchester; he was taken by Manchester as a schoolboy apprentice and bought up through the youth system at Manchester.

Therefore David Beckham does not fulfil the definition of an asset and is therefore not included in Manchester United's statement of financial position. However, if I had asked the question "Was Andrei Shevchenko an asset in Chelsea's statement of financial position?" the answer would have been yes as he meets the definition of an asset.

Shevchenko was included in Chelsea's statement of financial position as an intangible asset and amortised over the length of his initial contract.

2903

Some years ago a P2 exam included a scenario of a football club and one of the issues was the capitalisation of the player's transfer fee.

For both the F7 and P2 exams the examiners have given scenarios requiring understanding and recognition of an asset in a company's statement of financial position. It is a frequent area of both exams and something students must understand and be able to look at the scenario and decide whether or not an asset should be recognised in the financial statements.

As a parting shot, if Real Madrid, for example, were to buy all of Manchester United's equity shares and Manchester United were now a subsidiary of Real Madrid, would David Beckham now be recognised as an asset in Real Madrid's consolidated statement of financial position? The answer would now be yes.

General comments

✓ The performance of candidates on both sections was quite closely correlated.

SECTION A (MCQs)

✓ Cover as much of the syllabus as possible – therefore no area can be neglected in preparing for this exam.

Two questions that caused difficulty are reviewed below:

MCQ 3

Drexler acquired an item of plant on 1 October 2012 at a cost of $500,000. It has an expected life of five years (straight-line depreciation) and an estimated residual value of 10% of its historical cost or current cost as appropriate. As at 30 September 2014, the manufacturer of the plant still makes the same item of plant and its current price is $600,000.

What is the correct carrying amount to be shown in the statement of financial position of Drexler as at 30 September 2014 under historical cost and current cost?

	Historical cost ($)	Current cost ($)
A	320,000	600,000
B	320,000	384,000
C	300,000	600,000
D	300,000	384,000

Analysis

Less than a third of candidates got this answer correct. The **correct answer B** is worked out as:

Historical cost

Annual depreciation = $90,000 (($500 × 90%) ÷ 5)

After two years carrying amount would be $320,000 ($500 – (2 × 90))

Current cost

Annual depreciation = $108,000 (($600 × 90%) ÷ 5).

After two years carrying amount would be $384,000 ($600 – (2 × 108))

✗ Most candidates chose A or C. They did not appreciate that current list price needs to be depreciated to give an equivalent current value for a similar aged item.

✗ D was the least popular wrong answer; it ignored residual value when calculating depreciation based on historical cost.

MCQ 19

During the year ended 30 September 2014 Hyper entered into two lease transactions:

On 1 October 2013, a payment of $90,000 was made, being the first of five equal annual payments of a finance lease for an item of plant. The lease has an implicit interest rate of 10% and the fair value (cost to purchase) of the leased equipment on 1 October 2013 was $340,000.

On 1 January 2014, a payment of $18,000 was made, being for a one-year lease of an item of excavation equipment.

What amount in total would be charged to Hyper's statement of profit or loss for the year ended 30 September 2014 in respect of the above transaction?

A $108,000
B $111,000
C $106,500
D $115,500

Analysis

Observing the dates given, the finance lease charge is based on a full year and consists of both depreciation and the finance cost (interest) on the liability; the operating lease charge will be 9 months of the annual rental.

The correct answer is C:

	$
Depreciation of plant (340,000 ÷ 5)	68,000
Interest ((340,000 – 90,000) × 10%)	25,000
	93,000
Rent of equipment (18,000 × $^9/_{12}$)	13,500
Total charge to profit or loss	106,000

✗   The most common incorrect answer was A, which treated the cash flows (90,000 + 18,000) as the charge to profit or loss. This is **fundamentally wrong**!

✗   Incorrect answer B treated the leases correctly in principle, but **ignored** the time apportionment of the operating lease (93,000 + 18,000).

✗   Incorrect answer D treated the leases correctly in principle, but assumed the finance lease payment was in arrears rather than in advance (as stated).

! Read the question carefully!

SECTION B

✓ Most candidates answered all questions.

✗ A small number did not attempt Q1.

✗ Some candidates waste time and earn no marks:

> ➢ **not** reading the question thoroughly; or
> ➢ giving answers that were **not** required.

✗ Poor handwriting and illegible workings continues to be a major problem.

Question 1

This required analysis of a company targeted for acquisition. The target was part of a family group. The requirement was to adjust the accounts by eliminating preferential issues and then recalculate ratios. The ratios were then to be analysed in comparison with given ratios and industry averages.

✗ Some struggled to gross up cost of sales by 10% (figure given was 90% of the correct amount).

✗ Many calculated ROCE when ROE was asked for.

! Marks **cannot** be given for not answering the requirement.

✓ Although mistakes were made quite a few candidates achieved full marks for the recalculation of ratios.

✓ Some candidates scored quite well on part (b).

The main issue was that the recalculated ratios were much lower than the original ones.

✗ Marks **cannot** be awarded for simply stating that a ratio is lower or higher.

✓ Candidates must "dig" deeper into ratios and understand their meaning.

Question 2

This required the adjustment to a given profit and the preparation of a statement of financial position. Adjustments were required for the issue of a loan note, a revaluation, depreciation and tax.

✓ Candidates did quite well with this question.

The main problems concerned the required adjustments:

✗ Loan note issue cost were sometimes wrongly added to the proceeds rather than deducted. (If consequential calculations were correct no further marks were lost under "own figure rule".)

✓ Most dealt with the revaluation quite well **but** errors included ...

✗ omitting land from value of assets;

✗ depreciating land;

✗ not adjusting retained earnings for new depreciation;

✗ including revaluation surplus in retained earnings.

✓ Many candidates correctly calculated the movement in deferred tax **but** ...

    ✗ did not split it between profit or loss and other comprehensive income.

! **Read** what the question requires in respect of the movement in deferred tax. If it does **NOT** state that the full movement should be taken to profit or loss the split is **required**.

✗ Some candidates did not in effect answer (a), even though the calculations were done for (b).

! It is difficult to give marks if requirements are not followed. This is an example of **poor examination technique**.

Question 3

This required the preparation of a consolidated statement of profit or loss and other comprehensive income and the consolidated statement of financial position; with a 3 mark requirement on the treatment of the subsidiary's intangible assets in the consolidated statements.

The question tested the usual consolidation issues:

✓ fair value adjustments;

✓ intra-group trading with unrealised profits;

✓ cash in transit;

✓ intra-group loan; and

✓ goodwill impairment.

✓ Most had a good understanding of consolidation and were comfortable splitting profits into pre and post-acquisition.

✗ A number were unable to correctly calculate retained earnings at date of acquisition (opening retained earnings plus $^3/_{12}$ current year profits or closing retained earnings less $^9/_{12}$ current year profits).

Common mistakes included:

✗ Post-acquisition depreciation and unrealised profit treated as part of the goodwill calculation.

✗ Deducting 12 months' intra-group sales rather than 9 months.

✗ Calculating unrealised profit based on profit margin rather that profit mark-up. Some even treated the whole amount of inventory as unrealised!

✗ Ignoring post-acquisition depreciation.

✘ Deducting goodwill impairment from expenses rather than adding the expense.

✘ Inability to deal with the interest on the deferred consideration; only 9 months should have been expensed to profit or loss.

✘ Only the post-acquisition increase in the revaluation should have been included in other comprehensive income, it should not have been time apportioned.

✘ Many did not present a non-controlling interest figure in profit or loss and even more omitted from other comprehensive income.

Although errors tended to have a knock-on effect in the statement of financial position, candidates were not penalised for the subsequent effect of earlier mistakes.

Specific errors in the statement of financial position included:

✘ Incorrect share price used for purchase consideration.

✘ Incorrect treatment of the intra-group balances and cash in transit. Cash and bank balances of parent and subsidiary **cannot** be netted off and the cash in transit should have reduced the parent's overdraft.

✘ The effect of the share exchange (increasing parent's share capital and premium) was not dealt with correctly; some completely ignored it.

✘ Many could not distinguish the different treatment of non-controlling interest in profit or loss against the treatment in the statement of financial position.

Part (b) required a short discussion of the treatment of the subsidiary's in-process research costs and customer list:

✓ both should be recognised as intangible assets in the consolidated statement of financial position;

✓ thereby reducing the amount of goodwill recognised on acquisition.

Section A	June 2015	Dec 2014	Specimen
Conceptual and regulatory framework	5 MCQs	4 MCQs	5 MCQs
Accounting for transactions in financial statements	10 MCQs	8 MCQs	6 MCQs
Analysing and interpreting financial statements	2 MCQs	3 MCQs	5 MCQs
Preparation of financial statements	3 MCQs	5 MCQs	4 MCQs
Numerical/non-numerical items	8/12	10/10	7/13
Section B			
Marks for calculation/discussion	50/10	48/12	49/11
Interpretation	●	●	●
Preparation of financial statements	●	●	●
Consolidations	●	●	●
IAS 7 *Statement of Cash Flows*	●		
IAS 12 *Income Taxes*	●	●	●
IAS 16 *Property, Plant and Equipment*	●	●	●
IAS 17 *Leases*	●		
IAS 18 *Revenue Recognition* (now IFRS 15)			●
IAS 32 *Financial Instruments: Presentation*	●	●	●
IAS 33 *Earnings Per Share*	●		
IAS 37 *Provisions, Contingent Liabilities and Contingent Assets*	●		●
IFRS 9 *Financial Instruments*	●		●

SPECIMEN PAPER REVIEW

Section A

✓ Made up of 20 two mark multiple choice questions.

✓ On average students should give 3.6 minutes per question. Some questions may only take a few seconds but others may take longer than the average.

✓ Paper consists of 12 "theory" type questions and 8 "calculation" based questions.

✓ The areas covered by the questions are as follows:

> ➢ 4 × Consolidation
> ➢ 3 × Interpretation
> ➢ 2 × Framework
> ➢ 2 × IAS 17
> ➢ 2 × General
> ➢ 1 each of IASs 8, 10, 23, 33, 36, 38 and 41

✓ Ensure all questions are answered, there is no negative marking on MCQs, you are either right and will earn 2 marks or wrong and will earn no marks.

Section B

✓ Made up of two 15 mark questions and one 30 mark question, all are compulsory.

✓ 27 minutes should be allocated to the 15 mark questions and 54 minutes allocated to the 30 mark question.

Question 1

✓ 15 mark interpretation. 5 marks are allocated to calculation of ratios and 10 marks to the discussion. The question cannot be passed on ratios alone.

✓ Be selective in the ratios calculated, you must be able to refer to them in your answer.

✓ The scenario is based on the acceptance of a new contract and the impact the new contract will have on operating performance.

✓ There is guidance in the requirements in terms of what NOT to do, follow the guidance.

✓ Use the information given in the question to formulate the answer, be specific to the scenario set and do not deviate from the requirements.

Question 2

✓ 15 mark consolidation. Only extracted figures are required and not a full statement of financial position.

✓ This is all about using workings to good effect to calculate the four requirements of the question.

✓ Goodwill, non-controlling interest, property, plant and equipment and the equity section is all that is required.

✓ Use of the net asset schedule will assist in working towards those four requirements.

✓ Non-controlling interest is valued at fair value on acquisition; to arrive at reporting date value add a percentage of post-acquisition profits. There has been no impairment of goodwill.

✓ Ensure the purchase consideration is reflected, at present no action has been taken to record the consideration. It will impact on the equity position as well as the calculation of goodwill.

✓ Remember to include a figure for "consolidated other equity" in your solution.

Question 3

✓ Prepare financial statements from a trial balance and supporting notes and discuss the movement on property, plant and equipment.

✓ Similar to Q2 in old exam format, so ensure this style of questions is used for revision practice.

✓ Specific issues covered by this question include:

> Revenue
> Financial Instruments
> IAS 16
> IAS 37
> IAS 12

✓ Read the question thoroughly during the 15 minutes of RAPT and again when you start the question.

> Do not ignore the statement of changes in equity, there are three "easy" marks available. You will not lose marks if the figures are incorrect, as long as they are the same figures calculated previously ("own error rule").

EXAMINATION TECHNIQUE

Reading and Planning Time (RAPT)

✓ Try to rank the three questions in Section B according to their level of difficulty – plan to attempt the easiest first and the most difficult last.

✓ Although you may use your calculator during this time it is more effective to jot down your ideas for the written elements of Section B questions.

✓ Restrict calculations done in RAPT to those that do not need to be presented in your script as a working .

✓ Use any remaining time to start selecting correct answers for non-computational MCQs.

Time Allocation

✓ Allocate your time:

➢ 2-mark MCQs ≈ 3½ minutes each
➢ 15-mark Section B Qs ≈ 27 minutes
➢ 30-mark Section B Q ≈ 54 minutes

✓ Answer all questions.

✓ The first marks are the easiest to gain in Section B Qs, so always start the next question rather than overrun on the time allocation.

Multiple Choice Questions

✓ These objective questions mostly consist of:

⇒ a "stem" (the question);
⇒ a "key" (the correct answer);
⇒ 3 "distracters" (plausible but incorrect answers).

✓ Follow the following steps when answering a question:

⇒ read the question requirement, **in bold**;
⇒ write down or think about anything that might help you, such as a "T" account;
⇒ solve the question;
⇒ select the appropriate letter from the answer sheet.

Exam Advice

✓ Cover up the answers A, B, C, D when doing calculations. Remember:

➢ a "penultimate" calculation is likely to be a distractor;

➢ a disproportionate amount is more likely to be a distracter than the key.

✓ If getting close to the end of the time allocation for Section A and you still have a few questions left to answer – guess!

> ➢ If you have time at the end of the exam you can still come back and check them.

> ➢ Avoid leaving questions unanswered before you move to Section B as you will **not** be allowed to complete the MCQ answer sheet when the examine supervisor instructs you to stop writing.

Section B

Numerical requirements

✓ Before starting a computation, picture your route:

> ➢ Note down the steps needed; and
> ➢ imagine the layout of your answer.

✓ A columnar layout is often appropriate:

> ➢ it helps avoid mistakes; and
> ➢ is easier for the marker to follow.

✓ Write clearly and leave space, if you make a mistake you will then have room to insert the new figure..

✓ Include all your workings and **cross-reference** them to the face of your answer.

✓ State any assumption if necessary to progress with an answer – but it must **not** contradict the question.

✓ If you later notice a mistake in your answer, do **not** waste time amending the consequential effects of it:

> ➢ Clearly indicate where you have spotted it;
> ➢ you will not be penalised for errors caused by an earlier mistake (under the "own error" rule).

✓ If you cannot calculate something needed in a later step, make a sensible guess and continue (e.g. assume a return on capital employed and use this to analyse the results of a company).

Written requirements

✓ **Planning**

> ➢ Read the requirement carefully to identify:

> > – exactly what is required;
> > – the separate issues to be addressed;
> > – how many points you need to make.

> ➢ Note down *relevant* thoughts on your plan – this may be on the question paper.

> ➢ Give your plan a structure which you can follow when you write up the answer.

✓ **Presentation**

➢ Answers structured around headings and sub-headings are easier to read.

➢ Use short paragraphs for each point.

➢ Use bullet points if appropriate. Each bullet point **must** "read" on from an introduction to the list or be complete in itself.

✗ You must **not** write in "note form".

➢ Write legibly using a good quality **black** pen.

✓ **Style**

✗ Do **not** write an essay.

➢ More points briefly explained tend to earn more marks than one or two points detailed points.

➢ Where relevant give real life examples to support your comments.

➢ Appropriate comments on amounts that have been calculated incorrectly will be given credit.

➢ Similarly, relevant comments consistent with a sensible assumption you be awarded marks.

✗ Do **not** "knowledge dump".

ABOUT BECKER PROFESSIONAL EDUCATION

Becker Professional Education provides a single destination for candidates and professionals looking to advance their careers and achieve success in:

- Accounting

- International Financial Reporting

- Project Management

- Continuing Professional Education

- Healthcare

For more information on how Becker Professional Education can support you in your career, visit www.becker.com.